MARYLAND TRAVEL GUIDE 2023:

The accurate guide to exploring Maryland's hidden treasures with safety advice

Matthew E. Davis

All rights reserved. No part of this publication may be reproduced, distributed, or transmitted in any form or by any means, including photocopying, recording, or other electronic or mechanical methods, without the prior written permission of the publisher, except in the case of brief quotations embodied in critical reviews and certain other noncommercial uses permitted by copyright law.

Copyright © Matthew E. Davis, 2023.

Table of Contents

Introduction to Maryland
Making Travel Plans for Maryland
Means of Getting to Maryland
Exploring Baltimore, the Inner Harbor
Discovering and Exploring Annapolis
Exploring the Chesapeake Bay
Visiting Historic Sites and Landmarks
Nature Adventures in Maryland
Cultural Experiences in Maryland
Practical Tips and Safety Information

Chapter 1

Introduction to Maryland

Overview of Maryland

Sincerely speaking, Maryland is one of the US states that is both secure and enjoyable to go through. My first journey was early in the year 2023, and it was incredible. I was extremely impressed by the manner the people embraced me. In this lovely state, there are many things to discover. The museums, activities, places to drink and eat, and much more. As you learn and experience Maryland, this book in your palm will unquestionably be your finest travel companion.

The first thing you need know is that Maryland, or the State of Maryland as it is formally called, is a state in the Mid-Atlantic area of the United States. Along with Delaware and the Atlantic Ocean to the east, it shares borders with the states of Virginia, West Virginia, and Pennsylvania to the south, west, and north, respectively.

With a total size of 12,407 square miles (32,133 square kilometers), Maryland is one of the smaller states in terms of land area. It boasts the 19th greatest population of any state in the United States despite its tiny size.

The biggest city in the state and its capital, Baltimore, is also a significant economic and cultural center. Frederick, Rockville, Gaithersburg, and Bethesda are a few of Maryland's other significant cities.

With a combination of coastal plains, undulating hills, and the Appalachian Mountains in the western half of the state, Maryland offers a diversified topography. Maryland's topography is dominated by the Chesapeake Bay, which offers a substantial waterway and significantly influences the state's economy and culture.

Being one of the original thirteen colonies that made up the United States has given the state a rich history. In both the American Revolution and the War of 1812, it was of utmost importance. The national song of the United States, "The Star-Spangled Banner," was composed by Francis Scott Key in Maryland during the War of 1812.

The economy of Maryland is varied, with important roles played by industries including biotechnology, aerospace, military, healthcare, and information technology. The National Institutes of Health (NIH), the Food and Drug Administration (FDA), and the National Security Agency (NSA) are just a few of the significant government organizations based in the state.

The University of Maryland, College Park, the United States Naval Academy, and other esteemed universities are just a few of Maryland's world-famous educational institutions.

With attractions ranging from historic locations like Fort McHenry to natural beauties like the Chesapeake Bay and Assateague Island, the state provides a wide range of leisure possibilities. Crab feasts and seafood festivals are two prominent events in Maryland's thriving seafood culture.

Maryland features a bicameral legislature, an executive branch run by the governor, and a court system presided over by the Court of Appeals, the state's highest court.

Overall, Maryland is a distinct and thriving state in the United States due to its combination of a rich history, a varied economy, natural beauty, and cultural attractions.

Regional context

Maryland is situated in the American Mid-Atlantic area. Several states and bodies of water around it. The location of Maryland is broken out as follows:

- Neighboring States
- Virginia: Maryland and Virginia share a southern boundary. The Potomac River, which divides the two states, acts as the boundary.
- West Virginia: West Virginia and Maryland share a boundary to the west. The North Branch Potomac River and the Youghiogheny River form the boundary.
- Pennsylvania: Pennsylvania forms Maryland's northern boundary. The Mason-Dixon Line in the west and the tripoint in the east where Maryland joins Pennsylvania and Delaware are the two ends of the boundary.
- Delaware: Delaware and Maryland share the northeastern boundary. The boundary stretches

all the way to the Atlantic Ocean from the tripoint with Pennsylvania and Delaware.
- Water Bodies:
- Chesapeake Bay: The Chesapeake Bay, a sizable estuary that divides the state into eastern and western portions, is home to a sizeable chunk of Maryland. Maryland's topography is shaped significantly by the Chesapeake Bay, which also has a major effect on the state's economy and ecosystem.
- Atlantic Ocean: Maryland has a modest stretch of shoreline that runs along the ocean, mostly in the southeast. Popular tourist sites such as Ocean City are located along the shore.

- Important Cities
- Baltimore: Baltimore, the state's biggest city and a significant economic and cultural hub, is situated in the state's central region.
- Annapolis: Located on the Chesapeake Bay, Annapolis is the state capital of Maryland and is renowned for its historic allure and naval links.
- Columbia: A planned town noted for its high standard of living and diversified population,

Columbia is situated halfway between Baltimore and Washington, D.C.

- Frederick: Located in the state's western region, Frederick is a historic city renowned for its downtown area's preservation and closeness to the Appalachian Mountains.

Overall, the geography of Maryland includes a variety of coastal regions, interior rivers, rolling hills, and mountains, offering inhabitants and tourists a variety of vistas and recreational options.

Weather and Climate

Maryland has four distinct seasons and a diverse climate. Its weather patterns are influenced by its position along the US East Coast. Here is a summary of the weather and climate of Maryland:

- Summers: Maryland's summers are often warm and muggy. Mid-80s to low 90s Fahrenheit (approximately 29 to 34 degrees Celsius) are the typical high temperatures, with occasional heatwaves bringing those numbers up to upper 90s Fahrenheit (35 to 37 degrees Celsius). High humidity may occur, particularly in July and August.

- Winters: Maryland has chilly to cold winters, with typical high temperatures in the low to mid-fifties Fahrenheit (7 to 11 degrees Celsius). However, especially in January and February, low temperatures might occur. In the western and mountainous areas of the state, more substantial quantities of snowfall occur.

- Spring and Autumn: In Maryland, spring and autumn are seasons of change. Spring is characterized by moderate weather, with typical highs in the 60s to 70s Fahrenheit (15 to 25 degrees Celsius), and rising precipitation. With typical highs in the 60s to low 70s Fahrenheit (about 15-23 degrees Celsius), autumn is known for its pleasant weather. Maryland has stunning fall foliage, especially in the state's western region.

- Precipitation: Throughout the year, Maryland has a modest quantity of precipitation. Rainfall is spread pretty equally, with somewhat more falling in the summer. The amount of snowfall varies by location, with the western and mountainous regions receiving the most snowfall. During the Atlantic hurricane season, which normally lasts from June to November, tropical storms or hurricanes may have an influence on coastal areas.

It's crucial to remember that weather patterns may change from year to year and that extreme weather phenomena like blizzards and severe storms can happen. When traveling to or living in Maryland, it is wise to check the local weather predictions and be ready for seasonal changes.

Culture and History

1.4 Background

Early colonial times are the origin of the lengthy history of Maryland. Here are some crucial details:

- Colonial Period: A Catholic nobleman named Lord Baltimore (Cecilius Calvert) established Maryland as a proprietary colony in 1634. English Catholics who were persecuted in England were given shelter in the colony. Since the colony's Act of Toleration, passed in 1649, gave some protection for religious freedom, Maryland grew to be recognized for its tolerance of all religions.

- American Revolution: Maryland was a key player in the American Revolution. The state was strategically significant because of its proximity to the Chesapeake Bay. Francis Scott

Key was inspired to create "The Star-Spangled Banner," which subsequently became the national song of the United States, by the Battle of Baltimore in 1814, which took place during the War of 1812.

- Slavery during the Civil War: Slavery was a historical institution in Maryland. Maryland did not break away from the Union during the American Civil War (1861–1865) even though it continued to be a slave state. The state's loyalties were split, with some Marylanders fighting for the Confederacy and others for the Union.

- Industrialization and Urbanization: Maryland saw industrialization and urban expansion in the late 19th and early 20th centuries. Baltimore developed into a significant hub for commerce and industrial, notably in shipbuilding and steel manufacture. The city's seaport and accessibility to important highways helped it grow economically.

- Civil Rights Movement: Maryland went through the Civil Rights Movement in the 20th century, much like many other regions of the United States. In the struggle for equal rights, the state contributed to the desegregation of public places like schools.

1.5 Language:
The historical, geographical, and ethnic influences on Maryland's culture are varied. The following are some facets of Maryland culture:

- Cuisine: Blue crabs are Maryland's most well-known seafood delicacy. Local specialties include crab feasts and crab cakes. Steamed clams, oysters, and crab soup made in the manner of Maryland are some more regional fare. The Smith Island cake, a stacked cake with several thin cake layers and icing, is another specialty of the state.

- Sports: Football and lacrosse are especially popular in Maryland's vibrant sports culture. Football teams from the University of Maryland

Terrapins (NCAA) and the Baltimore Ravens (NFL) both have ardent followings. Lacrosse is a popular sport that is played both professionally and recreationally. The University of Maryland has a good lacrosse program.

- Festivals and Events: Throughout the year, Maryland holds a number of festivals and events. With jousting contests, historical attire, and entertainment, the Maryland Renaissance Festival, which takes place in Crownsville, provides a look into the Middle Ages. The Preakness Stakes, a prestigious horse racing competition that is a component of the Triple Crown, takes place every year in Baltimore.

- Arts and Culture: Maryland is home to a thriving arts community that includes theaters, museums, and art galleries. Popular cultural landmarks in Baltimore include the National Aquarium, Walters Art Museum, and Baltimore Museum of Art. The Maryland Symphony Orchestra, various theatrical groups, and music festivals are all located in the state.

- Historical Attractions: Maryland is home to several historical attractions, including Fort McHenry National Monument and Historic Shrine, where Francis Scott Key composed "The Star-Spangled Banner." the Harriet Tubman Underground Railroad National Historical Park, the Naval Academy in Annapolis, and the Antietam National Battlefield.

These are just a handful of Maryland's historical and cultural high points. The state's distinctive cultural character is influenced by its distinctive fusion of customs, historical importance, and various populations.

Notable Marylanders

numerous famous people who have had a big impact in numerous disciplines have called

Maryland home. These Maryland residents are well-known:

1. The words of "The Star-Spangled Banner," which became the national anthem of the United States, were written by lawyer and poet Francis Scott Key. He was born in Maryland's Carroll County.

2. Abolitionist and political activist Harriet Tubman was a key player in the Underground Railroad, a system that assisted enslaved African Americans in escaping to freedom. She was born in Maryland's Dorchester County.

3. Thurgood Marshall was the first African American to hold a position on the U.S. Supreme Court and a well-known civil rights attorney. High Court. Before being appointed to the Supreme Court, he worked on several important civil rights issues. He was born in Baltimore, Maryland.

4. Frederick Douglass: After escaping slavery and rising to prominence in the abolitionist movement, Frederick Douglass was a significant abolitionist, author, and orator. He lived in Maryland for a while before relocating to Baltimore.

5. Eleanora Fagan, better known by her stage name Billie Holiday, was a well-known jazz singer and composer who was noted for her distinctive vocal technique. Despite having grown up in Baltimore, Maryland, she was raised in Philadelphia, Pennsylvania.

6. Jada Pinkett Smith was born and reared in Baltimore, Maryland, and is an actress, producer, and singer best known for her work in "The Matrix" trilogy and "Girls Trip."

7. Babe Ruth: George Herman Ruth Jr., better known as Babe Ruth, was a renowned professional baseball player who excelled in hitting home runs. He started his career playing for the Baltimore Orioles after being born in

Baltimore, then moved on to the Boston Red Sox and New York Yankees.

8. John Waters: John Waters, a writer, visual artist, and director, was reared in Baltimore, Maryland, and is best known for his provocative and sometimes contentious movies like "Pink Flamingos" and "Hairspray."

9. Michael Phelps: With 23 Olympic gold medals, Michael Phelps is the most decorated Olympian of all time and a record-breaking swimmer. He was reared in Baltimore County, Maryland, where he was born.

10. Rachel Carson was a marine scientist and environmentalist whose book "Silent Spring" served as a catalyst for the development of the contemporary environmental movement. Although she was born in Springdale, Pennsylvania, she lived in Maryland for the most of her professional life.

These people are but a small sample of the many notable Marylanders who have achieved success in a variety of industries. A large number of skilled and famous individuals have come from Maryland as a result of the state's rich history and varied population.

Chapter 2

Making Travel Plans for Maryland

Ideal Season to Visit

Depending on your interests and the activities you have planned, there is no one optimum time to visit Maryland. Spring, summer, autumn, and winter are the four different seasons of Maryland. Here is a summary of the climate and hot events for each season:

1. Spring (March to May): Maryland has warm weather and floral blooms throughout the spring. If you prefer outdoor pursuits like hiking,

bicycling, and visiting nature areas, now is a fantastic time to go. Washington, DC's Cherry Blossom Festival. (close to the Maryland border) becomes a well-liked destination in late March or early April.

2. Summer (June to August): Maryland's summers are hot and muggy, but they also have a lot of sunlight. Beach vacations and water sports in the Atlantic Ocean or Chesapeake Bay are best at this time of year. During this season, you may partake in water activities, outdoor concerts, and seafood festivals.

3. Fall (September to November): Because of the pleasant weather and gorgeous foliage, fall is regarded as one of the greatest seasons to visit Maryland. The state is ideal for leaf-peeping and outdoor activities as its picturesque landscapes take on vivid hues of red, orange, and gold. The Maryland Renaissance Festival, which takes place in Crownsville, is a well-liked occasion at this time of year.

4. Winter (December to February): Maryland has frigid winters with occasional snowfall. You may visit destinations in the state's western region, including Wisp Resort, if you appreciate winter activities like skiing or snowboarding. Ice skating rinks, beautiful decorations, and festivities like the Baltimore Christmas Village all come with the holiday season.

As a result, it's always a good idea to check the forecast before your trip. It's vital to keep in mind that Maryland's weather may be unexpected. The ideal time to go may also depend on certain activities or sites you're interested in, so do your homework and make your plans accordingly.

Length of Stay in Maryland

The length of your stay in Maryland will vary depending on a number of variables, including your interests, the reason for your trip, and the things you want to do there. Here are some suggestions to think about while choosing the length of your stay:

1. Weekend break: A weekend vacation to Maryland might be fun if you're searching for a fast break or just have a short amount of time. In places like Baltimore or Annapolis, you may tour the major attractions, go to historic locations, take part in waterfront activities, and sample the local food. You should get a taste of all Maryland has to offer over a two- to three-day vacation.

2. A stay of three to five days might be appropriate if your main interest is in seeing a particular city, such as Baltimore or Annapolis, and being fully immersed in its culture, history, and attractions. You may explore local eating and nightlife alternatives, as well as museums, art galleries, and historic places, during this time.

3. Outdoor Activities and Nature: You may want to give your trip additional time if you want to participate in outdoor activities like hiking, camping, or touring state parks and natural regions. The Appalachian Mountains, the Chesapeake Bay, and Assateague Island are just a few of the breathtaking scenery in Maryland. To truly appreciate and delight in the outdoor pleasures Maryland has to offer, think about staying a week or longer.

4. Attending an Event or Festival: If your trip is focused on attending an event or festival, take into account how long it will last and if you'll need more time to explore the region. For the Preakness Stakes horse race in Baltimore, as an example, you could wish to schedule a weekend vacation that includes the race day and some extra sightseeing.

The best length of your stay in Maryland will ultimately depend on your interests and the particular activities you want to engage in. Consider your interests as you plan your schedule to make the most of your stay in this varied state with a variety of attractions.

Spending and Budgeting

Budgeting and prices for a vacation to Maryland might vary based on a number of variables, such as your preferred modes of transportation, lodging preferences, food alternatives, and planned activities. Here are some essential factors to keep in mind when you create your travel budget:

1. Accommodation: Depending on where you stay and the kind of housing you choose, lodging costs in Maryland might vary. Major metropolitan areas like Baltimore and Annapolis often provide a variety of lodging choices at various price ranges, including luxury hotels, mid-range hotels, and inexpensive lodging. In addition, there are accommodation choices

including hotels and vacation rentals. To locate alternatives that meet your budget, compare costs and do some research on various lodgings.

2. Depending on how you want to travel to and within Maryland, the cost of transportation will vary. Consider the cost of travel to important airports like Baltimore/Washington International Thurgood Marshall Airport (BWI) if you're flying in. In Maryland, there are public transportation choices including buses and trains that may make travelling around cities and adjacent regions more affordable. If you want more freedom or to visit rural regions, renting a vehicle can be essential, although it will increase your costs.

3. Dining: The price of your meal will vary depending on your tastes and the kind of restaurant you choose. Trying regional favorites like Maryland crabs or crab cakes may be a unique experience since Maryland is famed for its seafood. A variety of eating alternatives are available, including low-cost eateries, mid-range

restaurants, and expensive restaurants. Investigate neighborhood markets, food carts, or inexpensive casual dining choices to save money.

4. Activities and Attractions: There are numerous attractions and activities in Maryland, many of which charge admission. Do some research on the prices for the particular locations you want to see, such museums, parks, and historic sites. Also take into account any extra costs associated with any optional activities you may wish to participate in, such as boat trips, outdoor adventures, or special events.

5. Budget for supplemental costs, such as souvenirs, parking fees, tipping, and any extra entertainment or shopping you want to partake in while on your vacation.

Making a budget and estimating your costs for each of the aforementioned categories is a smart idea. You may keep under your chosen spending limit for your vacation to Maryland by doing some pricing research, evaluating your alternatives, and making advance plans.

Traveling records

Make sure you have the required travel papers before you go for Maryland. The following are the main papers you'll probably need:

1. Passport: If you're coming from another nation to Maryland, you'll need a current passport. Ensure that your passport is valid for at least another six months after the date of admission into the United States and that it is not expired.

2. Visa: You could require a visa to enter the United States depending on your nationality. Verify in the US. To find out whether you need a visa, see the Department of State website or contact the closest embassy or consulate of the

United States in your nation. If you do, be sure to submit your application well before your trip.

3. ESTA (Electronic System for Travel Authorization): Before going to the United States, people of nations qualified for the Visa Waiver Program, which permits quick trips for business or pleasure, must have their ESTA authorized. Make sure to submit your ESTA application on the official website at least 72 hours prior to your flight.

4. COVID-19 Requirements: Additional travel requirements and limitations can be in place as a result of the continuing COVID-19 epidemic. Visit the U.S. government's official websites. For the most recent travel warnings, visa restrictions, and health advice, see the Department of State and the Centers for Disease Control and Prevention (CDC).

5. Travel Insurance: Having travel insurance is not required, but it is recommended to do so in order to protect oneself from unforeseeable

events like trip cancellations, medical problems, or lost baggage. Examine several travel insurance choices and choose a plan that meets your requirements.

To make sure you have all the required travel papers, it is crucial to review the precise requirements for both your country of residency and any transit countries you may pass through. During your travel, keep your paperwork organized and accessible.

Keep in mind to often check for any revisions or modifications to the criteria for travel paperwork since they might change over time. the U.S. government's official websites. The most precise and recent information for traveling to Maryland will be provided by the Department of State and applicable immigration authorities.

Making Hotel Reservations

The following advice should be kept in mind while making hotel reservations for your trip to Maryland:

1. Compare and Research: Start by looking at various lodging possibilities in the Maryland regions you want to visit. Compare costs, read reviews, and check the facilities provided by various hotels, bed & breakfasts, vacation rentals, and other kinds of lodgings using travel websites, search engines, and online booking platforms.

2. Location: Take into account where your hotel is in relation to the sights or activities you want to check out. Look for lodging near to certain locations or landmarks if you wish to be close to them. Moreover, take into account elements like security, ease of access to public transit, and close food alternatives.

3. Budget: Establish your travel spending limit and use it to narrow your search. Remember that prices might change based on the time of year, the area, and the kind of lodging. Additionally, it is important to look into any specials, offers, or package packages that the lodging companies may be offering.

4. Consider the room or suite type that best meets your requirements and preferences while looking at room types and amenities. Do you require a family suite, many rooms for a party, or a single room? If Wi-Fi, parking, breakfast, exercise equipment, or a pool are vital to you, look for such amenities.

5. evaluations and Ratings: To obtain a sense of the quality and level of service offered by the lodging, read evaluations from past visitors. This might assist you in making a choice and preventing any future problems.

6. Booking Flexibility: Before making a reservation, review the cancellation conditions

and regulations. It might be advantageous to be adaptable in case your trip plans need to alter at the last minute.

7. Third-Party Platforms vs. Direct Booking: Think about making a direct reservation with the lodging provider since they could give better terms or discounts. However, third-party booking sites may also provide affordable pricing and comprehensible layouts for comparison.

8. Early Booking: It's always advised to book early if you have certain dates or accommodations in mind, especially during busy travel times or for major events, to secure your chosen lodging and maybe get lower pricing.

Keep a record of your reservation information, including any confirmation numbers. If you have any specific requests or inquiries prior to your arrival, it's also a good idea to get in touch with the lodging provider immediately.

You can choose the best lodging for your vacation to Maryland by doing extensive research, evaluating your alternatives, and taking into account your unique requirements and preferences.

Chapter 3

Means of Getting to Maryland

Airports in Maryland

There are many airports in Maryland that provide both domestic and international service. Major airports in Maryland include the following:

1. The biggest and busiest airport in Maryland is Baltimore/Washington International Thurgood Marshall Airport (BWI), which is situated in Linthicum not far from Baltimore. With over 27 million people served yearly, it provides a large selection of local and international flights.

2. Although it is legally in Arlington, Virginia, Ronald Reagan Washington National Airport (DCA) is conveniently situated in Maryland and serves the Washington, D.C. metropolitan region. It is renowned for its closeness to Washington, D.C.'s center and mostly provides domestic flights.

3. Washington Dulles International Airport (IAD) is a significant airport that serves the Washington, D.C., metropolitan region. It is located in Dulles, Virginia. Although it isn't officially in Maryland, it's close by and has both domestic and international flights.

4. General aviation and charter flights are the main focuses of Hagerstown Regional Airport (HGR), which is situated near Hagerstown, Maryland. Compared to the large international airports described above, it is smaller in size.

5. The eastern coast of Maryland is served by Salisbury-Ocean City Wicomico Regional

Airport (SBY), which is located in Salisbury, Maryland. It serves general aviation needs and provides a few commercial flights.

These are a few of Maryland's major airports. You may choose the most practical airport for your trip based on your unique travel requirements and final destination.

Options for Ground Transportation

For moving throughout the state and to and from the airports in Maryland, there are a number of ground transportation choices. Here are a few typical choices:

1. Taxis and ridesharing services are extensively accessible in Maryland, including Uber and Lyft. Using a smartphone app, you may quickly order a trip or hail a cab. While rideshare services may

pick you up from any area, taxis are often located at designated taxi stands.

2. Shuttles: To get visitors to and from the airport, many hotels, particularly those close to airports, provide shuttle services. It is recommended to confirm with your hotel in advance if they provide these services and whether there are any related costs.

3. Public transportation: Maryland, especially the Baltimore-Washington metropolitan region, boasts a robust public transit system. Bus, light rail, and subway services are run by the Maryland Transit Administration (MTA) in the Baltimore region, whilst the Metrorail and Metrobus services are run by the Washington Metropolitan Area Transit Authority (WMATA) in the Washington, D.C., region.

4. Rental cars: There are several automobile rental businesses operating in Maryland if you'd like to have your own mode of transportation.

There are rental vehicle services at major airports and in other locations around the state.

5. Private vehicle Services: For individualized transportation, you may engage private vehicle services like limos or car service businesses. These services provide a better degree of comfort and convenience but are often more costly than taxis or rideshares.

6. Trains: Baltimore Penn Station, BWI Marshall Rail Station, and New Carrollton Station are just a few of the train stations in Maryland that are run by Amtrak, the nation's rail service. Amtrak connects Maryland to other states through regional and long-distance rail service.

When selecting a ground transportation option in Maryland, it's crucial to take into account elements like price, convenience, and the precise region you're going.

Maryland's public transportation

There are several public transit alternatives in Maryland for getting throughout the state. Several of Maryland's main public transit networks are listed below:

1. The Baltimore metropolitan area's public transportation system is run by the Maryland Transit Administration (MTA). Local bus services, Metro SubwayLink, and Light RailLink are all included. Convenient transit options inside Baltimore City and to the neighboring suburbs are offered by the Light RailLink and Metro SubwayLink.

2. Although the Washington Metropolitan region Transit Authority (WMATA) mainly serves the Washington, D.C. metropolitan region, Metrorail and Metrobus services are also provided throughout Maryland. Montgomery County and Prince George's County are only two of the counties in Maryland that are connected to

Northern Virginia and Washington, D.C. through the Metrorail subway system.

3. Services for Commuter Buses: The Maryland Transit Administration (MTA) runs commuter bus services that link different parts of Maryland to the Washington, D.C. metropolitan area. These buses are designed to carry commuters to and from work during periods of heavy traffic.

4. MARC Train: The Maryland Area Regional Commuter (MARC) train service links Maryland with surrounding states, notably Washington, D.C., and areas of West Virginia and Pennsylvania. Three lines—the Penn Line, Camden Line, and Brunswick Line—are used by MARC trains.

5. Local Bus Services: Several counties in Maryland run their own local bus systems in addition to the MTA and WMATA bus services. These bus services provide transit inside certain counties and sometimes also have connections to other regions.

6. Regional Transportation Agencies: There are regional transportation agencies that provide public transportation services in certain regions of Maryland in addition to the aforementioned networks. For instance, TheBus and Howard Transit both operate in the counties of Prince George's and Howard, respectively.

It's crucial to confirm the times, routes, and costs of the particular public transportation services you want to utilize since they could change. Additionally, transit tickets or cards could be offered to provide frequent passengers economic discounts.

Maryland drivers' license

Driving in Maryland is typically simple, but there are a few important considerations to make if you want to do so:

1. Driving: If you are a resident of another state or nation visiting Maryland, you may drive with your current driver's license. However, if you want to live in Maryland, you must apply for a license within 60 days after moving there.

2. Before driving in Maryland, familiarize yourself with the state's traffic rules and regulations. To guarantee your safety and prevent fines or penalties, observe speed limits, traffic signs, and signals, as well as all other traffic rules.

3. Seat Belts: In Maryland, everyone riding in a car must wear a seat belt. All passengers, including the driver, must use seatbelts or be buckled into a suitable child safety seat.

4. mobile Phone Use: In Maryland, using a hand-held mobile phone while operating a motor vehicle is prohibited. If you need to make or receive calls while driving, you must utilize hands-free equipment or Bluetooth technology.

5. kid Safety Seats: Depending on the kid's age, weight, and height, Maryland has varied regulations for child safety seats. If you are traveling with children, make sure you are aware of and follow these rules.

6. Speed restrictions: Depending on the kind of road and area, different speed restrictions apply. Observe the specified speed limits and alter your speed as necessary. Unless otherwise indicated, the speed limit in residential zones is typically 25 mph.

7. Toll highways: Maryland contains a number of toll highways, bridges, and tunnels, including the Intercounty Connector (ICC) and the Chesapeake Bay Bridge. Cash, E-ZPass (an electronic toll collection system), or other acceptable payment methods are all acceptable ways to pay for tolls. While some toll booths are automated, some are manned.

8. Parking: When parking your car, pay close attention to the rules and signs. While residential neighborhoods may have permit parking limitations, parking meters or dedicated parking structures may be accessible in metropolitan areas.

9. Winter driving: The winter weather that Maryland encounters may have an impact on the state's roads. In the winter, be ready for slick or snowy roads and drive carefully. It's a good idea to have a snow scraper, chains, snow tires, and emergency supplies in your car.

10. Drunk driving: In Maryland, it is against the law to operate a vehicle while under the influence of drugs or alcohol. The permitted blood alcohol content (BAC) is 0.08%. If you intend to drink, choose an alternate mode of transportation or assign a sober driver.

When driving in Maryland, proceed with care, abide by the rules of the road, and pay attention to other road users. To guarantee a safe and comfortable driving trip, familiarize yourself with the particular laws and regulations of the regions you want to visit.

Bus and Train Services

Transport options inside Maryland and to its neighbors include a number of rail and bus services. Here are a few of the most popular bus and rail options:

1. MARC Train: The Penn Line, Camden Line, and Brunswick Line are the three lines that make up the Maryland Area Regional Commuter (MARC) train service. Baltimore, Harford County, Howard County, and Montgomery County are just a few of the Maryland counties that are connected to Washington, D.C. and other areas in the region by MARC trains. With minimal service on weekends, the trains run throughout the week.

2. Amtrak: Amtrak runs a number of railway terminals in Maryland and is the country's main rail provider. Baltimore, Aberdeen, and New Carrollton in Maryland are connected to Boston, Washington, D.C., Philadelphia, and other East Coast cities by the Northeast Corridor line. Regional and long-distance rail services are both provided by Amtrak.

3. Bus service provided by the Maryland Transit Administration (MTA) is extensive and services the Baltimore metropolitan area as well as areas nearby. The bus lines go across a number of counties, including Carroll, Anne Arundel, Harford, Howard, and Baltimore County. Within these regions, MTA buses provide easy transit.

4. Bus: The Washington Metropolitan region Transit Authority (WMATA) runs Metrobus services that reach into Maryland, while it mainly serves the Washington, D.C., metropolitan region. Montgomery County, Prince George's County, and other Maryland

counties are serviced by Metrobus lines that link them to the wider Washington, D.C. metropolitan area.

5. Commuter Buses: The Maryland Transit Administration (MTA) runs commuter bus services that link different parts of Maryland to the Washington, D.C. metropolitan area. These buses provide easy transportation for persons who work in or around Washington, D.C. since they are designed expressly to carry commuters during peak travel hours.

6. County and City Bus Services: In Maryland, many counties and cities may each provide a unique local bus service. These bus services, like Howard County's Howard Transit or Prince George's County's TheBus, provide transportation within certain geographic areas. They provide services to nearby villages and might link to them.

It's a good idea to research the timetables, routes, and costs of the individual rail and bus services you want to use while making travel plans. While some services allow cash or contactless payment options, others may demand advanced ticket purchase or the usage of fare cards.

Chapter 4

Exploring Baltimore, the Inner Harbor

Discovering Inner Harbor

Baltimore, Maryland's Inner Harbor is a well-known tourist destination and a historic seaport. There are many different entertainment, eating, shopping, and cultural opportunities in this crowded waterfront neighborhood. The Inner Harbor's main characteristics and attractions are listed below:

1. National Aquarium: One of the great attractions of Baltimore's Inner Harbor is the National Aquarium. Numerous interactive

displays are available, such as a walk-through rainforest and a multi-level shark tank, and it is home to thousands of marine animals.

2. Maryland scientific Center: The Maryland Science Center is an interactive scientific museum including planetarium presentations, an IMAX cinema, and interactive exhibits. It is a terrific destination for both kids and adults and covers a broad variety of scientific fields.

3. Historic Ships: There are a number of well-preserved historic ships in the Inner Harbor that you may explore, including the USS Constellation, a cruiser from the Civil War, the USCGC Taney, a Coast Guard cutter from World War II, and the USS Torsk, a World War II submarine.

4. These two nearby shopping areas, Harborplace and The Gallery, include a wide selection of retail establishments, shops, dining options, and food vendors. It's a terrific location

for souvenir shopping, dining with a harbor view, or just taking a leisurely walk.

5. Waterfront Promenade: There is a lovely promenade that runs the length of the waterfront in the Inner Harbor. It provides beautiful harbor views, proximity to a number of sights and landmarks, and is an excellent spot to stroll or run.

6. The Inner Harbor is well-known for staging dragon boat races, a well-liked water activity in which teams paddle long, slender boats adorned with dragons. The races are held yearly and draw competitors from all around the globe.

7. Events & Festivals: Throughout the year, the Inner Harbor plays home to a number of festivals and events. These include the Light City Festival, the Chesapeake Crab & Beer Festival, the Light City Festival (a light and art spectacular), and many more.

8. Cruises aboard the Spirit of Baltimore are an option if you'd want to see the harbor from the sea. Dining, entertainment, and breath-taking views of the city skyline and waterfront are all included on these trips.

Overall, Maryland's Inner Harbor is a bustling tourist spot that mixes history, entertainment, and scenic beauty. It is a must-visit place in Baltimore since it provides a broad variety of attractions and activities that are catered to various interests and age groups.

National Aquarium

One of the top tourist destinations in the region is the National Aquarium, which is situated in Baltimore, Maryland's Inner Harbor. Here are some of the National Aquarium's main attributes and highlights:

1. displays: The aquarium has a huge selection of displays that display a diversity of marine life from all around the globe. You may visit several ecosystems to discover creatures like sharks, dolphins, turtles, jellyfish, and vibrant tropical fish, such as tropical rainforests, coral reefs, and the Amazon River.

2. Blacktip Reef: A large, immersive exhibit that depicts the ecology of an Indo-Pacific coral reef is one of the National Aquarium's most well-liked displays. There are many blacktip reef sharks, colorful coral structures, and other fish species there.

3. Dolphin Discovery: The National Aquarium has a display of Atlantic bottlenose dolphins called Dolphin Discovery. Learn about dolphin behavior and conservation at the exhibit's educational lectures and hands-on activities.

4. In a theater that blends 3D pictures with sensory sensations like wind, mist, and vibrations, the aquarium's 4D Immersion Theater

lets visitors see short films about marine life. It offers a distinctive and interesting method to discover the underwater environment.

5. Animal Encounters: The National Aquarium offers visitors the chance to interact closely with a few of the creatures. Touch tanks where you may engage with and learn about marine life, such as stingrays and horseshoe crabs, may be one of these interactive experiences.

6. The aquarium is dedicated to promoting environmental awareness and conservation. To safeguard marine habitats and advance sustainable practices, they take part in several research and conservation initiatives. Visitors may discover more about these programs and how they support ocean conservation.

7. The National Aquarium organizes a variety of special events and activities throughout the year, including animal encounters, behind-the-scenes tours, and sleepovers for various age groups. These occasions provide one-of-a-kind chances

to interact with marine life and discover more about the aquarium's conservation initiatives.

It's a wonderful voyage into the realm of aquatic life to visit the National Aquarium, where you can discover the value of preserving our seas and experience a variety of ecosystems. People of all ages and interests will find it to be a fun and instructive experience.

USS Constellation

Baltimore, Maryland's Inner Harbor is home to the historic cruiser USS Constellation. The USS Constellation's salient characteristics and details are listed below:

1. History: The USS Constellation, a sloop-of-war, is the only warship from the Civil War period still in existence. It was commissioned in 1855 and participated in a variety of military engagements, mostly in the

seas off the coasts of the Mediterranean, Africa, and South America.

2. Preservation: To bring the USS Constellation back to her former look, substantial restoration work was done in the 1990s. The ship was restored with the goal of presenting visitors with an authentic experience of naval history by faithfully recreating her look during the Civil War era.

3. Tours: The USS Constellation is open for guided tours for visitors to the Inner Harbor. These excursions provide an opportunity to view the ship's many decks, staterooms, and living spaces. Knowledgeable tour guides tell fascinating anecdotes about the ship and her crew in addition to providing historical background.

4. exhibitions: The USS Constellation is home to enlightening exhibitions that provide details about the ship's past, sailors' everyday life, and historical naval activities. To improve the tourist

experience, the exhibits include interactive displays, photos, and artifacts.

5. Reenactments and Events: From time to time, the USS Constellation holds reenactments and special events that give guests the chance to see historical performances and get a glimpse of life aboard a 19th-century cruiser. These activities provide a special chance to become acquainted with the ship's past and bygone nautical customs.

6. Education: The USS Constellation provides educational opportunities for tourists and students of all ages. These programs attempt to include participants in practical activities including knot-tying lessons, sail-hoisting exercises, and sailor-life simulations on historic ships.

7. Waterfront Setting: With the USS Constellation docked in the Inner Harbor, tourists may examine the ship and take in the harbor vistas in a lovely setting. It is handy to visit numerous places in the region since it is

close to other attractions including the National Aquarium and the Maryland Science Center.

The USS Constellation provides insight into the Civil War era's use of naval warships as well as the rich maritime history of the United States. For history buffs and others interested in the history of the navy, exploring the ship and learning about its intriguing past offers a distinctive and instructive experience.

Maryland Science Center

Baltimore, Maryland's Inner Harbor is home to the Maryland Scientific Center, a well-known scientific museum. The Maryland Science Center's salient characteristics and details are listed below:

1. displays: The science center provides a broad selection of engaging displays that span many scientific fields. The earth, space, physics,

chemistry, and biology are just a few of the subjects that visitors might research. Visitors may learn via interactive displays and experiments since the exhibits are intended to be interactive and fun.

2. IMAX Theater: The Maryland Science Center has an IMAX Theater where entertaining and informative movies are shown on a huge screen. The theater's immersive sound system and high-resolution images provide a unique cinematic experience. The videos cover a wide range of topics, such as science, space exploration, and environment.

3. The scientific center has a planetarium that presents engrossing presentations about astronomy and the night sky. Immersive displays that mimic starry sky, planetary motions, and astronomical events are available to visitors. The planetarium programs provide enlightening perspectives on the cosmos and beyond.

4. Scientific Encounters: The Maryland Science Center offers visitors the chance to take part in real-time scientific experiments and demonstrations. These Science Encounters provide engaging demonstrations and interactive lectures by science instructors that highlight scientific ideas.

5. The science center contains a section specifically designated for younger visitors called the Kids Room. With age-appropriate displays and activities that encourage scientific research and curiosity, this area is intended for hands-on learning.

6. Special exhibits: The Maryland Science Center often presents transient exhibits. These specialized exhibits often investigate cutting-edge scientific research and technical breakthroughs or concentrate on certain scientific topics. They provide visitors the chance to learn more about certain branches of science.

7. Programs for Education: The scientific center provides a range of educational programs for individuals, families, and school groups. These initiatives consist of science-themed seminars, summer camps, and other activities that promote inquiry-based learning and pique interest in the natural world.

8. Observation Deck: The Maryland Science Center's top level has an observation deck that provides sweeping views of the Inner Harbor and the surrounding area's urban landscape. From this vantage point, visitors may take in breath-taking views of Baltimore's skyline and harbor.

People of all ages may explore and learn about many scientific subjects at the Maryland Science Center in a fun and interactive setting. It is a well-liked location for both residents and visitors interested in science and exploration because of its interactive displays, educational activities, and immersive experiences.

Historic Ships

Several historically significant ships that have been kept well may be seen in Baltimore, Maryland's Inner Harbor, giving tourists a window into the nautical past. You may tour the following famous historic ships in the Inner Harbor:

1. The final remaining warship from the Civil War period is a sloop-of-war named USS Constellation. It mostly operated in the oceans of the Mediterranean, Africa, and South America. The ship is open for visitors to explore, take guided excursions, and learn about its history.

2. The only surviving vessel that was there during the assault on Pearl Harbor in 1941 is the USCGC Taney, a United States Coast Guard cutter that saw action during World War II. You may visit the ship and discover more about how

it participated in maritime operations during the conflict.

3. USS Torsk: The USS Torsk, a Tench-class submarine that saw action in World War II, is renowned for destroying the Japanese ship Amakusa, the war's last enemy ship. The control center, living quarters, and torpedo chambers are all accessible for visitors to see.

4. Lightship Chesapeake: Also referred to as LV 116, the Lightship Chesapeake served as a floating lighthouse that directed ships in the Chesapeake Bay. Step on board to discover the significant contribution lightships provide to marine navigation.

5. Seven Foot Knoll Lighthouse: For more than a century, the Seven Foot Knoll Lighthouse served as a historic screw-pile lighthouse on the Chesapeake Bay. It was moved to the Inner Harbor and is now accessible for excursions. Visitors may go to the summit and take in the waterfront views.

This rare chance to live on ancient ships that have major roles in maritime history is made possible by these ships. Insights into the difficulties encountered by sailors, the technology employed, and the naval activities of their various periods are provided via guided tours and exhibitions. The ancient ships of the Inner Harbor are worth a visit whether you're interested in naval history, maritime heritage, or just appreciate seeing unusual ships.

National Monument and Historic Shrine at Fort McHenry

In Baltimore Maryland, there is an important historical site called Fort McHenry National Monument and Historic Shrine. It honors Fort McHenry's contribution to the War of 1812, notably its performance in the Battle of Baltimore in September 1814.

About the Fort McHenry National Monument and Historic Shrine:

1. Historical Importance: By successfully defending Baltimore Harbor from British naval bombardment during the War of 1812, Fort McHenry played a crucial role. Francis Scott Key was inspired to create "The Star-Spangled Banner," which subsequently became the national song of the United States, by the Battle of Baltimore and the fort's tenacity.

2. National Monument and Historic Shrine: On March 3, 1925, Fort McHenry received the designation of national monument and historic shrine. The National Park Service (NPS), which oversees its management, protects the fort and its environs as a representation of American patriotism and national identity.

3. Fort McHenry is a star-shaped bastion fort constructed of stone and brick. It has sweeping

views of the neighborhood and is perched on a peninsula that faces Baltimore's Inner Harbor. The fort's many buildings, including as the barracks, powder stores, and famous flagpole where the Star-Spangled Banner was hoisted, are open for visitors to examine.

4. Visitor Center and displays: Visitors may learn more about the Fort McHenry's War of 1812 history via interactive displays and historical context at the Fort McHenry Visitor Center. The national anthem's inspiration flag, war memorabilia, and multimedia displays are all on display in the exhibits.

5. Flag rituals: Every day at Fort McHenry, flags are raised and lowered during rituals that replicate the hoisting of the Star-Spangled Banner. These events, which are backed by a military band, are well-liked by tourists.

6. Outdoor Recreation: The Fort McHenry National Monument and Historic Shrine has nearby parklands that provide options for

outdoor pursuits in addition to the fort itself. Picnicking, strolling along the waterfront promenade, and admiring the picturesque vistas of the port and the Chesapeake Bay are all enjoyable activities for visitors.

7. Events and Programs: Throughout the year, the location holds a variety of events and programs, including presentations by rangers, living history demonstrations, and special commemorations of American history and the War of 1812.

8. Visitor facilities: To accommodate visitors of all abilities, the national monument provides visitor facilities such a gift store, picnic spots, bathrooms, and accessible features.

It's a rare chance to learn about American history and understand the importance of the War of 1812 by going to Fort McHenry National Monument and Historic Shrine. It serves as a symbol of American perseverance and a source of pride for the country.

Camden Yards and the Museum of Sports Legends

In Baltimore, Maryland, Camden Yards and the Sports Legends Museum are two interwoven attractions that honor the city's long history in sports, notably baseball.

1. Camden Yards: The Baltimore Orioles, the city's Major League Baseball franchise, play their home games in the renowned baseball complex known as Camden Yards. It was built in 1992 and is renowned for its retro-modern style, which incorporates elements of ballparks from the early 20th century. Camden Yards revived the movement toward creating stadiums with a more conventional aesthetic, which had an impact on the style of later sporting arenas.

2. Retro-Modern Architecture: By integrating vintage features like a brick facade, steel trusses, and an asymmetrical field layout, Camden Yards ushered in a new era of stadium architecture. The design of the stadium and the close-quarters seating arrangement produced an exciting and fan-friendly atmosphere that brought fans closer to the action.

3. facilities and Features: The stadium provides guests with a wide range of facilities, including a selection of seating choices, opulent suites, dining establishments, concession stands, and distinctive view spots like the flag court and Eutaw Street. Between the field and the Sports Legends Museum, on Eutaw Street, there are pregame celebrations, food carts, and baseball memorabilia that are well-known.

4. Sports Legends Museum: Adjacent to Camden Yards, the Sports Legends Museum is devoted to preserving and promoting Maryland's sporting heritage. The museum features a variety of sports, but it primarily emphasizes the heritage

of Baltimore baseball, including the Orioles and the Baltimore Black Sox of the Negro Leagues.

5. Exhibits and Artifacts: The Sports Legends Museum offers engaging exhibits, displays, and artifacts from illustrious players, teams, and occasions. Exhibits on baseball legends including Babe Ruth, Brooks Robinson, Cal Ripken Jr., and many more are available for visitors to explore. The museum highlights the state's rich athletic history by covering a variety of other sports, including as football, lacrosse, and horse racing.

6. Educational and Interactive Programs: The museum provides interactive activities, led tours, and educational programs for guests of all ages. It offers a thorough grasp of the sports culture in Maryland and the influence of local players on the domestic and worldwide scene.

7. Combined Experience: Fans may get the whole sports experience by visiting both Camden Yards and the Sports Legends Museum.

They may go to an Orioles baseball game at the stadium, study the Sports Legends Museum's history and exhibits, and even go out and about in the neighborhood, which is home to additional attractions like the Babe Ruth Birthplace and Museum.

Baseball aficionados, sports enthusiasts, and anybody interested in the history of Maryland's sports culture should visit Camden Yards and the Sports Legends Museum. You will be immersed in the rich history of Baltimore's sports legacy whether you are watching a game or touring the museum.

Visiting Walters Art Museum

A famous art museum with a vast collection spanning thousands of years and several civilizations is called the Walters Art Museum and is situated in Baltimore, Maryland. It is renowned for having a wide variety of artworks, including ornamental arts, jewelry, manuscripts, paintings, and sculptures.

1. History and Architecture: Henry Walters, a well-known art collector and philanthropist, founded the Walters Art Museum in 1934. The museum is situated in an opulent edifice that includes three historic buildings: the original 19th-century estate of William T. Walters, the nearby mansion of his son Henry Walters, and a contemporary 1974 addition.

2. Collection: The museum's collection consists of more than 36,000 items that span many different time periods, including the ancient worlds of Asia, Byzantium, medieval Europe, and Egypt. A vast variety of creative materials, such as paintings, sculptures, pottery, textiles, jewelry, and illuminated manuscripts, are available for visitors to examine.

3. Highlights: The Walters Art Museum is home to a number of noteworthy pieces of art and

artifacts. Highlights include the "Walters' Art of Asia" collection, which showcases fine Asian art, the "Chamber of Wonders," which displays treasures from the Renaissance and the Middle Ages, and the "Egyptian Mummies" collection, which features mummies and other artifacts from ancient Egypt.

4. Renaissance and Baroque Art: Of special interest is the museum's collection of Renaissance and Baroque artwork. Masterworks by well-known European painters including Botticelli, Titian, El Greco, Rembrandt, and Vermeer may be found there. These outstanding masterpieces' beauty and workmanship are visible to visitors.

5. Special exhibits: The Walters Art Museum often presents transient exhibits that provide a more in-depth look at certain subjects, historical eras, or artists. These shows often feature loans from other organizations and private collections, giving viewers a one-of-a-kind and stimulating experience.

6. Conservation and Research: The museum is committed to the preservation of its collection and academic research. There is a cutting-edge conservation lab there where specialists strive to restore and preserve artworks in order to ensure their long-term preservation.

7. Education and Programs: For visitors of all ages, the Walters Art Museum provides educational programs, seminars, lectures, and guided tours. These programs provide chances for education, participation, and a greater comprehension of the shown works of art.

8. Amenities: The museum offers a number of conveniences, such as a café, a gift store, and a lovely outdoor sculpture garden where visitors may relax and take in the scenery.

The Walters Art Museum provides a fascinating trip through time and civilizations that enables guests to understand the variety and magnificence of human creation. It is a cultural treasure in Baltimore that welcomes art lovers, academics, and anybody looking for creative inspiration.

Neighborhoods in Fells Point and Canton

In Baltimore, there are two thriving and storied neighborhoods: Fells Point and Canton. These areas provide a distinctive fusion of culture, food, shopping, and entertainment and are renowned for their beautiful atmospheres, waterfront settings, and rich histories.

1. Fells Point: Situated on the southern side of Baltimore Harbor, Fells Point is a historic waterfront area. It has a particular marine tradition and stretches back to the 18th century. Old-world beauty is created by the cobblestone streets, brick rowhouses, and quaint stores.

2. Age-Old Charm: Fells Point is widely known for its beautifully restored older buildings. The Robert Long House, Baltimore's oldest house, is one of several structures in the area that are included on the National Register of Historic Places. Restaurants, shops, and art galleries are housed in beautifully renovated buildings that guests may wander around and appreciate.

3. Dining and Nightlife: With a variety of restaurants, Fells Point is a culinary destination. Visitors may indulge in delectable meals and enjoy the exciting nightlife at establishments serving seafood and crab, as well as foreign cuisines and modern gastropubs. The area is renowned for its plethora of pubs, live music venues, and quaint taverns that provide a vibrant ambiance.

4. Waterfront Promenade: Fells Point's waterfront position offers a beautiful backdrop. A leisurely stroll down the promenade, admiring the port, and even boarding boat cruises or water

taxis to see the neighborhood are all options for visitors.

5. Canton: Another well-liked waterfront area in Baltimore, Canton is close to Fells Point. Although it has a more residential vibe, the combination of restaurants, pubs, and stores still creates a vibrant ambiance.

6. Patterson Park: Patterson Park, a 137-acre urban park that offers plenty of room for outdoor activities, is one of the primary attractions in Canton. There are walking paths, playgrounds, sports fields, and even a pagoda with sweeping city views for visitors to enjoy.

7. First Thursday: Fells Point and Canton are well recognized for their neighborhood activities, and First Thursday is one of the most well-liked. Every month on the first Thursday, there is live music, art displays, food sellers, and special offers from neighborhood businesses.

8. Festivals & Events: Both Fells Point and Canton have a number of festivals and events that honor the regional culture throughout the year. The Fells Point Fun Festival, Privateer Day, and the Baltimore Dragon Boat Challenge are a few noteworthy occasions.

Fells Point and Canton districts provide a riveting experience for locals and tourists alike, whether you're wanting to explore the historic charm, eat delectable food, take in waterfront vistas, or immerse yourself in the local culture.

Chapter 5

Discovering and Exploring Annapolis

Visiting the U.S. Naval Academy

In the Maryland city of Annapolis, there is the United States Naval Academy (USNA). Future officers for the US Navy and Marine Corps are educated and trained at this esteemed college. Here are some important facts about the USA. Naval College

1. The Naval Academy is the second-oldest of the five military academies in the United States, having been established in 1845. The U.S. approved of its formation. Congress should

discuss the need for a specific navy school to educate midshipmen.

2. The goal of the navy Academy is to mold young people into skilled navy officers who uphold the greatest standards of devotion, bravery, and honor. The school places a strong emphasis on academic achievement, career advancement, and physical health.

3. Entry: Entrance into the United States. The Naval Academy has a strict admissions process. In addition to completing academic, physical fitness, and medical requirements, prospective midshipmen must also secure nominations from members of Congress or other recognized sources. This is all part of a rigorous application procedure.

4. Curriculum: A four-year undergraduate curriculum leading to a Bachelor of Science degree is available at the Naval Academy. Numerous disciplines from the arts, sciences, engineering, and social sciences are included in

the curriculum. Midshipmen also get military instruction while they are at the school.

5. Leadership and Character Development: The Naval Academy puts a high priority on these two areas. Midshipmen go through a thorough leadership development curriculum that equips them with the skills necessary to assume command and make decisions in the Navy and Marine Corps.

6. Brigade of Midshipmen: The Naval Academy's student body is referred to as the Brigade of Midshipmen. Around 4,400 midshipmen, both male and female, reside on campus at Bancroft Hall, one of the biggest dorms in the whole world.

7. In addition to their academic studies, midshipmen take part in a variety of training programs, including as summer voyages on military ships, where they get hands-on training in seamanship, navigation, and other naval operations.

8. Sports: The Naval Academy has a long history of competitive athletics, and playing varsity sports is a significant component of midshipmen's curriculum. The academy plays NCAA Division I football and belongs to the Patriot League.

9. Midshipmen are commissioned as ensigns in the Navy or second lieutenants in the Marine Corps once they graduate. After that, they continue to serve as officers, assuming different leadership and service positions within their respective military branches.

The Maryland-based U.S. Naval Academy has a long and illustrious tradition of developing strong, moral leaders for the United States. Marine Corps and the Navy. It is famous for its demanding academic curriculum, thorough military instruction, and dedication to producing future officers of character.

The Old City of Annapolis

In Annapolis, Maryland, there is a quaint and noteworthy neighborhood known as the Historic Annapolis District. It includes the city's historic downtown, which is renowned for its intact colonial architecture, extensive history, and diverse cultural heritage. Here are some of the district's main characteristics and highlights:

1. Beautiful colonial-era architecture serves as the district's defining feature. As you stroll around the streets, you'll see attractive row homes, Georgian-style mansions, and cobblestone pathways that give you a feel of the city's early days.

2. Historic Landmarks: The neighborhood is home to a number of significant historical sites. Here is where the Maryland State House is, the oldest state house still in use for legislative purposes. It is the location of the ratification of

the Treaty of Paris, which declared the American Revolutionary War to be over. The William Paca House, the Charles Carroll House, and St. Anne's Episcopal Church are more notable buildings.

3. The Historic Annapolis District's hub is the City Dock neighborhood in Annapolis. Visitors may wander around the harbor, take in beautiful views of the Chesapeake Bay, and see yachts and sailboats at this waterfront neighborhood. The port is flanked by stores, eateries, and cafés and serves as a focal point for a number of leisure pursuits.

4. Historic Sites and Museums: The area is home to a large number of historical sites and museums that highlight the legacy and history of Annapolis. Examples include the Banneker-Douglass Museum, the Annapolis Historic District Visitors Center, and the Annapolis Maritime Museum. These sites give historical insights into the city via its displays, artifacts, and educational activities.

5. The United States Naval Academy is situated in the Historic Annapolis District, as was already noted. The academy's presence enhances the district's historical importance and adds to its lively environment. The Naval Academy Museum, the academy's grounds, and the everyday activities and training of midshipmen may all be explored by visitors.

6. Events and Festivals: Throughout the year, the Historic Annapolis District conducts a number of events and festivals. Events like the Annapolis Boat Shows draw enthusiasts from all over the globe since Annapolis is regarded for having a vibrant sailing and boating culture. The area frequently hosts parades, concerts, and fireworks to mark important holidays like Independence Day.

7. Shopping and eating: The area provides a wonderful eating and shopping experience. Visitors may discover specialty businesses, art galleries, antique shops, and quaint cafés on

Main Street and Maryland Avenue. The region is well-known for its seafood establishments, where you may savor fresh crabs from the Chesapeake Bay and other regional specialties.

Visitors have the chance to get immersed in the city's colonial history via the Historic Annapolis District, see its historical sites, and take part in its nautical customs. This neighborhood provides a distinctive and unforgettable experience, regardless of your interests in history, culture, or just taking in the picturesque coastline.

Maryland State House

In Annapolis, Maryland's Historic Annapolis District, the Maryland State House is a noteworthy historical site. As the oldest state capital in continuous legislative use in the United States, it is very significant historically and architecturally. The Maryland State House's salient features are as follows:

1. Historical Significance: The Maryland State House was significant in shaping early American history. George Washington relinquished his position as commander-in-chief of the Continental Army in the Old Senate Chamber of the State House in 1783, upholding the fundamentals of civilian leadership of the armed forces. The Treaty of Paris, which recognized the United States as an independent country, was also approved in the State House in 1784.

2. Architecture: The State House is a stunning illustration of Georgian design. Joseph Horatio Anderson, an architect, designed it, and it was built between 1772 and 1779. White columns, a red-brick facade, and a sizable wooden dome—at the time, the biggest wooden dome ever built without nails in the United States—are some of the building's distinguishing characteristics.

3. Maryland State House Museum: The Maryland State House Museum is housed inside

the State House and provides exhibits and displays that shed light on Maryland's history, its contribution to the nation's formation, and the state's political development. The State House is highlighted with relics, records, and interactive displays that allow visitors to learn about significant occasions and individuals.

4. Legislative Chambers: The Maryland General Assembly, the state's legislative body, meets at the State House. The Senate and House of Delegates have their separate sessions in the building's respective chambers. When the General Assembly is in session, attendees may observe sessions to see the legislative process in action.

5. The Old Senate Chamber, which sits on the second level, is very significant historically. It has been kept to reflect how it looked at the time when George Washington resigned his commission, and it is the chamber in question. The room is furnished with antiques and has

pictures of notable Maryland historical personalities.

6. William Paca Garden is a painstakingly preserved colonial garden next to the State House that is named after William Paca, one of the Declaration of Independence's signatories. The garden offers a serene hideaway in the middle of Annapolis with its lovely flowers, plants, and ambience.

The Maryland State House is a monument to the state's lengthy history and its role in the founding of the United States. For individuals interested in colonial history and the founding of the country, it is a must-visit destination because to its historical importance, architectural beauty, and link to important events in American history.

William Paca House and Garden

Historic Annapolis District in Annapolis, Maryland is home to the William Paca House and Garden. Visitors may get a look into the way of life and beauty of the colonial period at this beautifully restored 18th-century home and garden. The William Paca House and Garden's most significant facts are listed below:

1. William Paca: A key player in Maryland's history and a signer of the Declaration of Independence was William Paca. He was the third governor of Maryland and a renowned jurist and politician. He lived at the William Paca House from 1765 till his passing in 1799.

2. The William Paca House is a magnificent example of Georgian architecture. William Buckland, an architect, is credited with its exquisite proportions, delicate woodwork, and excellent workmanship. Visitors may experience the way of life of the colonial aristocracy thanks

to the thorough restoration of the home to reflect its former splendour.

3. Historic Interiors: The house's interiors are decorated with antique furniture, paintings, and decorative items that reflect the period's fashion and aesthetic preferences. The drawing room, dining room, and bedrooms are just a few of the areas that guests may visit to get a look into the Paca family's lavish lifestyle and everyday routine.

4. Garden: The mansion is surrounded by the magnificent two-acre William Paca Garden. It is regarded as one of the best representations of an English-style garden from the 18th century in the country. The garden is decorated with symmetrical and geometric patterns, vivid flowers, and well trimmed hedges. It has a kitchen garden with herbs and vegetables, a fish-shaped pond, a summerhouse, and terraced grass.

5. Educational Activities: Visitors of all ages may participate in a variety of educational events and activities at the William Paca House and Garden. The site's history, architecture, and horticulture are all covered in guided tours. Additionally, seminars, lectures, and special events that dive deeper into colonial-era subjects are organized by the museum's staff and volunteers.

6. Preservation Initiatives: Historic Annapolis, a nonprofit organization devoted to the protection of historic structures in Annapolis, took up the restoration and preservation of the William Paca House and Garden. Their efforts have made sure that this important part of history is preserved and available to the general public.

You may go back in time by visiting the William Paca House and Garden and taking in the opulence and allure of colonial Annapolis. It provides a rare chance to see a historically significant property that has been exquisitely conserved and to take in the tranquil beauty of an actual 18th-century garden.

St. Anne's Church

In Annapolis, Maryland's Historic Annapolis District, there is a historic Episcopal church called St. Anne's Church. As one of the country's oldest still in operation churches, it is very noteworthy both architecturally and historically. Following are some significant facts regarding St. Anne's Church:

1. History: Since its founding in 1692, St. Anne's Church has had a long and rich history. At first, a brick church was erected there where a wooden one had already stood. The cathedral has seen many significant occasions throughout the years, such as religious services, political rallies, and memorial ceremonies for famous people.

2. The church's architecture is a lovely fusion of several architectural styles. Its initial building was a tiny, straightforward brick church, but during its history, it underwent several extensions and alterations. The existing structure is mostly of Georgian design, with subsequent additions of Gothic Revival and Victorian architecture.

3. St. Anne's Church is significant historically because it was a focal point of the political and religious life of Annapolis and Maryland. It functioned as the first Anglican church in the state and was where the first American bishop of the Episcopal Church was consecrated in 1784.

4. Cemetery: The graves of a number of famous people, including members of illustrious Maryland families, Revolutionary War soldiers, and signers of the Declaration of Independence, are interred in a historic cemetery next to the church. The cemetery offers a window into

Annapolis' history and a tranquil setting for thought and remembering.

5. Worship Services and Community: St. Anne's Church is still a busy place of worship and a thriving center of the neighborhood. The church has regular religious services and provides a range of activities, such as educational workshops, musical performances, and neighborhood outreach projects.

6. Preservation: Over the years, St. Anne's Church has been meticulously conserved and maintained. To retain its architectural integrity and preserve its historic elements, restoration work has been done. The church is a significant landmark in the Historic Annapolis District and is listed on the National Register of Historic Places.

It is possible to connect with Annapolis' past while learning about its architecture at St. Anne's Church, and you can also experience the continuing spiritual and communal life there. It is evidence of the continuing legacy of religion and the contribution of religious organizations to the formation of the local cultural landscape.

Maritime Museum of Annapolis

In the Maryland city of Annapolis' Historic Annapolis District, there is a cultural center called the Annapolis Maritime Museum. It is committed to preserving and displaying the nautical history of Annapolis and the surrounding area of the Chesapeake Bay. The Annapolis Maritime Museum's salient characteristics are as follows:

1. History and Location: The McNasby Oyster Company building, which housed a seafood packaging facility in the early 20th century, is now home to the Annapolis Maritime Museum. The museum building is a historic edifice, and its setting on Back Creek's banks provides stunning views of the river.

2. displays and Collections: The museum has a number of displays that examine the Chesapeake Bay region's marine history, ecology, and customs. The environment of the bay and its effects on commercial fishing are among the topics that tourists may learn about. The museum also has hands-on exhibits, models, relics, and images that vividly depict maritime history.

3. The Annapolis Maritime Museum provides educational activities and events for visitors of all ages. These programs include lectures, seminars, hands-on activities, and guided excursions that help participants gain a greater appreciation for the maritime past and the value of environmental stewardship.

4. Barge House and Park: The Barge House, a multipurpose venue utilized for exhibitions, events, and community meetings, is next to the museum. Visitors may relax, take in the scenery, and learn about the local ecosystem via

informative exhibits and natural habitats in the nearby park area.

5. Waterfront Activities: The museum actively engages with the neighborhood's marine culture. Visitors may explore Back Creek and the Chesapeake Bay thanks to its educational programs, boat cruises, and kayak rentals. The nature of the bay and the significance of its preservation are experienced personally via these activities.

6. Environmental advocacy: The Annapolis Maritime Museum is committed to advancing sustainability and environmental responsibility. It works with several groups to raise awareness of the problems the Chesapeake Bay is experiencing and to promote its preservation and rehabilitation.

7. Special Events: Throughout the year, the museum conducts a variety of special events, including marine festivals, art exhibitions, live music performances, and educational seminars.

These celebrations provide opportunities for community involvement while honoring the marine traditions and culture of the area.

The Chesapeake Bay and Annapolis' extensive nautical history are accessible via the Annapolis nautical Museum. It cultivates an understanding of the ecological, history, and cultural importance of the bay via its displays, educational programs, and community activities. The museum provides an educational experience for visitors of all ages, regardless of their interests in environmental protection, maritime history, or just taking in the waterfront scenery.

Harbor and City Dock

In the heart of Annapolis, Maryland, lies a bustling waterfront district called The City Dock and Harbor. It acts as a hub for leisure pursuits including boating, eating, shopping, and cultural events. The City Dock and Harbor's most important facts are listed below:

1. Setting on the water: The Annapolis Harbor's head, which links to the Chesapeake Bay, is where the City Dock is located. A lovely and energetic environment is produced by the magnificent waterfront site, which provides stunning views of sailboats, yachts, and historic structures.

2. Dockside Activities: Year-round events abound in the City Dock area. Visitors may enjoy the cool wind, take leisurely strolls along the docks, and observe the activity on the water. It's a nice spot to unwind, observe people, and take in the nautical ambience.

3. Boating and sailing: The City Dock and Harbor area in Annapolis, which is referred to as the "Sailing Capital of the United States," is the center of this nautical culture. Boaters may hire kayaks, paddleboards, and sailboats to explore the waters themselves, and the port is crowded

with yachts and sailboats. The region also holds major sailing competitions like the Wednesday Night Sailboat Races and the Annapolis Sailboat Show.

4. Cafes and restaurants: There are several eating alternatives available at the City Dock and Harbor. There are several eateries, cafés, and waterfront bars where patrons may savor local cuisine, fresh seafood, and outdoor eating with lovely harbor views. It's a wonderful location to have a meal or unwind with a drink while admiring the marine scenery.

5. Shopping and boutiques: There are many different types of stores and boutiques in the vicinity of the City Dock. Visitors may look through art galleries, upscale apparel boutiques, gift shops, and businesses with nautical themes. The stores provide a variety of handcrafted goods from the area as well as products with marine themes.

6. Cultural and celebratory activities are often held in the City Dock and Harbor region. Numerous activities, such as art festivals, live music performances, boat displays, and holiday festivities, happen all year round. The Annapolis Arts Week, the First Sunday Arts Festival, the Annapolis Oyster Roast, and the Sock Burning are noteworthy occasions.

7. Annapolis City Dock Park: The City Dock neighborhood has a small park where guests may relax on seats, have a picnic, and take in the views of the river. The park serves as a meeting spot for both residents and tourists, offering a peaceful haven among the bustling waterfront.

In Annapolis, the City Dock and Harbor provide a distinctive fusion of maritime history, leisure activities, dining, shopping, and cultural events. The City Dock and Harbor provide a charming and unforgettable waterfront experience, whether you're taking a walk along the docks, dining al fresco, or engaging in nautical sports.

The Eastport District

On the eastern side of the Annapolis Harbor in Annapolis, Maryland, the Eastport area is a thriving and historic neighborhood. Eastport provides a distinctive and one-of-a-kind experience, and is well-known for its maritime history, attractive streets, and bustling environment. The following are some significant facts concerning the Eastport area:

1. Eastport has a rich maritime history since it formerly had a large population of fisherman, boat builders, and sailors. The area is well renowned for having a close relationship with the Chesapeake Bay and the sea. The Eastport Yacht Club and Eastport nautical Museum are significant organizations that honor and preserve the local nautical heritage.

2. Eastport has a calm, nautical atmosphere that is evident. The area has a distinctive personality thanks to the streets being dotted with adorable cottages, vibrant row homes, and waterfront residences. Due to the abundance of marinas, boatyards, and docks in the region, there is a thriving and active boating community.

3. Dining and entertainment: Eastport is renowned for its vibrant entertainment choices and diversified food scene. The area is home to a variety of eateries, seafood stands, and waterfront pubs where guests may savor delectable seafood, picturesque waterfront views, and live music. Seafood crab houses, oyster bars, and informal restaurants are among the locals' favorites.

4. City Dock Access: The Spa Creek Bridge provides easy access from Eastport to the City Dock area and downtown Annapolis. Visitors may enjoy the best of both areas by taking a quick stroll or bike ride over the bridge to reach the busy City Dock.

5. Eastport-Annapolis Neck Park: In Eastport, there is a park known as Eastport-Annapolis Neck Park. It provides walking trails, parks, and sports fields so that locals and guests may engage in outdoor activities. The park also serves as a venue for neighborhood gatherings and sports leagues, strengthening the feeling of community in the area.

6. Events & Festivals: Eastport is well-known for its exciting festivals and neighborhood gatherings. Local bands and artists get together for the annual Eastport-A-Rockin' music festival, which features a day of live entertainment. The Tug of War, an Eastport custom, is a friendly contest between Eastport and downtown Annapolis teams that serves as a representation of the neighborhood's fierce rivalry.

7. Eastport has a strong feeling of belonging and pride in its community. Residents take an active involvement in neighborhood activities, volunteer projects, and civic organizations. The

Eastport Civic Association promotes the needs of the neighborhood's inhabitants while working to maintain the neighborhood's distinctive identity.

With its nautical history, picturesque streets, and vibrant waterfront community, the Eastport area in Annapolis provides a distinctive and exciting experience. Eastport offers a warm and lively environment for locals and tourists alike, whether you're exploring the neighborhood restaurants, going to festivals, or taking in the waterfront scenery.

Chapter 6

Exploring the Chesapeake Bay

Assateague Island National Seashore

On the American Atlantic coasts of Maryland and Virginia sits the Assateague Island National Seashore, a protected region. It is a barrier island that spans along the shore for around 60 kilometers (37 miles). The coast is renowned for its immaculate beaches, varied animals, and distinctive environment.

The following are some of the main characteristics and details of Assateague Island National Seashore:

1. Geographically speaking, Assateague Island is split into two halves. Assateague Island National Seashore, which is maintained by the National Park Service, is responsible for the island's northern two-thirds, which are situated in Maryland. The U.S. manages the island's southern part, which is located in Virginia. Chincoteague National Wildlife Refuge is managed by the Fish and Wildlife Service.

2. Animals: Assateague Island is well-known for its wild horses, sometimes referred to as Chincoteague ponies or Assateague horses. These horses are a top draw for tourists and are allowed to wander the island. Other animals that live on the island include ducks, migrating birds, foxes, deer, and foxes.

3. Beaches: Popular for swimming, tanning, and beachcombing, the seaside provides lovely sandy beaches. Visitors may explore the dunes and coastal woodlands in addition to taking in the unspoilt natural beauty of the shoreline.

4. Outdoor Activities: Assateague Island National Seashore offers a variety of activities for enjoyment. In authorized places, visitors may go camping, hiking, biking, and fishing. In the nearby bays and marshes, kayaking, canoeing, and paddleboarding are popular water sports.

5. Camping: For those who wish to spend the night, the seaside has various campsites. Reservations are advised, particularly during the busiest times of the year, at the campsites, which provide both tent and RV camping choices.

6. On Assateague Island, there are two visitor centers—one in Maryland and one in Virginia. These facilities include educational activities for visitors of all ages, information about the park, and displays on the area ecosystem and fauna.

7. Assateague Island is a protected region, thus there are rules in place to conserve its natural resources. Visitors must adhere to these rules, which could include limitations on dogs,

bonfires, off-road vehicles, and camping policies.

8. Additional attractions are available in the region around Assateague Island. Horses are herded over the canal for the yearly pony swim in the adjacent town of Chincoteague, Virginia. The community also has restaurants, shopping, and boat cruises.

A trip to Assateague Island National Seashore offers the chance to take in the unspoiled coastal scenery, see animals up close, and participate in a variety of outdoor activities. To maintain the preservation of this distinctive ecosystem, it is essential to preserve the natural environment and adhere to the rules.

Maritime Museum of the Chesapeake Bay

In St. Michaels, Maryland, which is near the Chesapeake Bay, there is a museum called the Chesapeake Bay Maritime Museum (CBMM). It focuses on the area around the Chesapeake Bay's rich maritime history and legacy. The museum provides displays, educational programs, and activities that highlight the history, customs, and environment of the bay.

Here are some of the Chesapeake Bay Maritime Museum's salient characteristics and details:

1. The museum's many displays explore various facets of the nautical history of the Chesapeake Bay. These exhibitions include interactive displays, historical boats, relics, and photos. Visitors may find out about the ecosystem of the bay, boatbuilding customs, the oystering and crabbing businesses, and navigational methods.

2. Historic Buildings: The 18-acre waterfront complex that makes up the CBMM is home to a

number of historic buildings. These buildings, which include a lighthouse, a functional boatyard, a shipwright's shop, and a seafood processing facility, provide visitors a comprehensive understanding of the area's nautical heritage. These structures are open to the public, who may also see demonstrations of traditional boatbuilding methods.

3. antique boats: Visitors to the museum are welcome to tour a collection of antique Chesapeake Bay boats. Traditional wooden sailing vessels, workboats, and pleasure boats all fall under this category. The boats provide information on the many kinds of boats used in the bay for transportation, entertainment, and fishing.

4. Programs for Education: The CBMM provides a variety of educational activities for visitors of all ages. These programs include sailing lessons, boatbuilding workshops, and practical lessons on Chesapeake Bay ecology and conservation. Additionally, the museum

offers year-round special events, summer programs, and school field excursions.

5. Events & Festivals: The museum hosts a number of celebrations of the history, customs, and culture of the Chesapeake Bay. The yearly Chesapeake Bay Maritime Festival, which offers live music, boat excursions, regional cuisine, and family-friendly activities, is one of the most well-liked occasions. Additionally, the museum conducts talks, exhibitions of art, and boat races.

6. Waterfront Activities: CBMM offers tourists the chance to participate in waterfront activities. The museum offers boat excursions, sailing lessons, and charters on its collection of vintage vessels that are now afloat. Visitors may learn about sailing methods, explore the bay's waters, and take in the beautiful scenery.

7. Waterfowl Festival: The CBMM is connected to this yearly celebration of waterfowl that takes place in Easton, Maryland. The event emphasizes the protection of waterfowl and their

habitats while showcasing animal art, such as paintings, sculptures, and carvings.

The Chesapeake Bay nautical Museum provides a unique opportunity to discover the nautical history of the bay, participate in interactive activities, and take in the natural beauty of the water and its ecosystems. The museum offers a thorough insight into the illustrious nautical traditions of the Chesapeake Bay area, whether you're interested in history, boatbuilding, ecology, or just spending a day on the water.

Visiting Historic St. Michaels District

In the Maryland hamlet of St. Michaels sits the beautiful and lovely St. Michaels Historic District. The historic area, which is located on the Eastern Shore of the Chesapeake Bay, is well-known for its intact 19th-century architecture, nautical history, and charming small-town ambience. Visitors may tour the town's historical sights and landmarks and get a look into its history.

Here are some details and significant characteristics of the St. Michaels Historic District:

1. Architecture: The area is known for its historic structures, the most of which were built in the 18th and 19th centuries. Colonial, Federal, and Victorian architectural styles are all present. Visitors may wander around the streets of the town and take in the well-kept houses, churches, and other buildings, which provide an understanding of the history and tradition of the community.

2. Talbot Street: Talbot Street is St. Michaels' principal road and the center of the city's historic quarter. It provides a lively ambiance and a variety of conveniences for tourists along with being lined with stores, restaurants, and galleries. Some of the buildings on the street

date back to the early 1800s, maintaining the street's historic beauty.

3. Despite being just beyond the St. Michaels Historic District's formal limits, the Chesapeake Bay nautical Museum (CBMM) is a vital component of the community's nautical legacy. The Chesapeake Bay region's history and culture are preserved and shown at the museum. It is a key attraction that helps to illuminate the town's maritime history.

4. Historic Landmarks: There are a number of significant historical sites in the St. Michaels Historic District. The St. Michaels Harbor, where tourists may see yachts, sailboats, and other boats, is one of the most famous. The St. Michaels Museum in St. Mary's Square, which has exhibits on regional history and the town's part in the War of 1812, is another notable site.

5. Events & Festivals: Throughout the year, St. Michaels conducts a number of events and festivals that enhance the historic district's

dynamic personality. The St. Michaels Wine Festival, which honors regional vineyards and provides tastings, is one of the most well-known occasions. The St. Michaels Brewfest, the Antique & Classic Boat Festival, and the St. Michaels Christmas festival are other events.

6. Activities on the Waterfront: The town's proximity to the Chesapeake Bay offers a range of waterfront activities. Visitors may join beautiful boat trips to take in the natural beauty of the region and see animals, or they can hire kayaks, paddleboards, or sailboats to explore the bay.

7. Dining and shopping options abound in the St. Michaels Historic District, where a variety of eateries, coffee shops, and bakeries provide delectable seafood delicacies from the Chesapeake Bay and other dishes. Additionally, tourists may peruse quaint boutiques, art galleries, and antique stores to uncover one-of-a-kind treasures and locally made goods.

A lovely fusion of history, architecture, maritime heritage, and small-town charm can be found in the St. Michaels Historic District. The neighborhood offers a remarkable experience for travelers interested in experiencing a little of the rich cultural legacy of the Chesapeake Bay, whether they're interested in visiting the historic buildings, indulging in delectable food, or enjoying waterfront activities.

Discovering Island of Tilghman

Known for its natural beauty, maritime heritage, and laid-back atmosphere, Tilghman Island is a small, picturesque island in Talbot County, Maryland, in the United States. It provides visitors with a tranquil retreat and a window into the distinctive culture and way of life of the Chesapeake Bay.

Here are some of Tilghman Island's salient characteristics and details:

1. Tilghman Island is located on Maryland's Eastern Shore, flanked by the Choptank River and the Chesapeake Bay. It may be reached by automobile from the mainland via a brief bridge. The island's seclusion and tranquility are enhanced by its isolated position.

2. Water sports and fishing: Tilghman Island has a long history of fishing, and many locals work as watermen. Visitors may explore the Chesapeake Bay's abundant waters by taking part in fishing charters and boat trips, seeing traditional crabbing and oystering practices, or both. Other water activities including sailing, kayaking, and boating are also popular on the island.

3. The island is well-known for its stunning scenery and unspoiled natural beauty. Spectacular vistas of the Chesapeake Bay, sunsets over the water, and an abundance of

animals are all available to visitors. The picturesque wetlands, farms, and charming waterfront houses on the island add to its pastoral appeal.

4. Seafood enthusiasts can find paradise on Tilghman Island. It has several top-notch waterfront eateries and seafood stands where you may have access to fresh, locally caught seafood such Maryland blue crabs, oysters, clams, and rockfish. Visitors may savor delectable seafood delicacies while seeing the shoreline.

5. Tilghman Island Museum: For those who are interested in the history and culture of the island, a trip to the Tilghman Island Museum is a must. The museum has displays on the island's fishing and boatbuilding customs, as well as the way of life of the local watermen and its distinctive ecology. It provides details on the island's history and the difficulties the locals have endured.

6. Outdoor Activities: Tilghman Island provides chances for outdoor activities in addition to fishing and water sports. Visitors may go birding, hike the island's natural paths, or picnic and sunbathe on its beautiful beaches. The serene atmosphere of the island is ideal for regeneration and relaxation.

7. Festivals and Events: Each year, Tilghman Island has a number of festivals and events to honor its customs and culture. A well-liked occasion with live music, seafood samples, boat excursions, and regional arts and crafts is the Tilghman Island Seafood Festival, which takes place in October. Another celebration that celebrates the island's sense of belonging and maritime history is Tilghman Island Day.

8. Accommodations: Despite being a tiny town, Tilghman Island has a variety of lodging options for tourists, including quaint bed & breakfasts, vacation homes, and beachfront inns. Visitors may completely immerse themselves in the

island's laid-back lifestyle and scenic surroundings by staying there.

An genuine and distinctive view of the Chesapeake Bay may be seen on Tilghman Island. Tilghman Island provides a pleasant and soothing vacation, no matter whether you want to learn more about the island's fishing history, savor some fresh seafood, or just find a quiet escape among stunning natural scenery.

Calvert Museum of the Sea

On the banks of the Patuxent River near Solomons, Maryland, lies a museum called the Calvert Marine Museum. It focuses on the natural history and cultural legacy of the Chesapeake Bay area, with a concentration on paleontology, marine life, and maritime history. Visitors of all ages may engage in activities, educational events, and exhibitions at the museum.

Following are some of the Calvert Marine Museum's salient characteristics and details:

1. The museum has a number of displays that examine the environmental and cultural history of the Chesapeake Bay. The bay's unique marine life, which includes fish, crabs, oysters, and other species, is available for visitors to learn about. The exhibits provide insights into the ecology of the bay via the use of live animal displays, interactive exhibits, and educational panels.

2. Paleontology: The museum's collection of fossils from the Chesapeake Bay area is one of its centerpieces. Visitors may see prehistoric whale bones, shark teeth, and other marine fossils. The paleontology display in the museum highlights the long history of the bay and how it has changed over the course of millions of years.

3. The Drum Point Lighthouse, a historic lighthouse that formerly helped ships navigate the Chesapeake Bay, is housed in the Calvert Marine Museum. The lighthouse is open for tours, and guests may learn about its significance for nautical navigation. The lighthouse offers a beautiful perspective of the nearby river and landscape.

4. Watercraft and Boat Tours: The museum provides rides on boats on the Patuxent River. To explore the bay's waterways and discover the area's nautical history, guests may join a vintage buyboat or a river cruise ship. Visitors may also explore a variety of old and fake boats at the museum.

5. Education and events: Visitors of all ages may participate in educational activities and events at the Calvert Marine Museum. These activities range from interactive displays to seminars, led tours, and nature hikes. Throughout the year, the museum also holds a variety of other events, talks, and workshops.

6. Skates and Rays: The Skates and Rays exhibit is one of the museum's distinctive displays. These intriguing animals, which are indigenous to the waters of the Chesapeake Bay and its surroundings, are available for visitors to see and learn about. The exhibit offers a chance to get a close-up look at these aquatic creatures and learn about their biology and behavior.

7. nautical History: The museum highlights the area of the Chesapeake Bay's extensive nautical history. Exhibits on the history of commercial fishing, the oystering and crabbing industries, and boatbuilding customs are available for visitors to explore. The museum also showcases relics, models, and images that chronicle the maritime history of the harbor.

8. Solomons Island: The Calvert Marine Museum is situated in the lovely hamlet of Solomons Island, which also has marinas, restaurants, and stores along the shore. Visitors may take in the picturesque vistas, visit nearby

art galleries, and experience delectable seafood in the lively ambiance of the town.

For anyone curious in the natural history, paleontology, and maritime legacy of the Chesapeake Bay, the Calvert Marine Museum offers an interesting and instructive experience. The museum provides a thorough investigation of the distinctive environment of the bay as well as its cultural value with its varied exhibits, interactive displays, and waterfront position.

Chapter 7

Visiting Historic Sites and Landmarks

Antietam National Battlefield

In the United States, Antietam National Battlefield is a historical monument close to Sharpsburg, Maryland. The American Civil War's Battle of Antietam, which took place on September 17, 1862, is preserved there. A startling number of people died during the conflict, making it the deadliest day in American history.

One of the earliest national battlefield parks in the United States, Antietam National Battlefield was created in 1890. The battlefield itself, as well as memorials, historical buildings, and monuments, are all included inside the roughly 3,200-acre park.

The Union Army of the Potomac, commanded by General George B. McClellan, and the Confederate Army of Northern Virginia, under the command of General Robert E. Lee, engaged in combat at Antietam. The conflict's significant turning point occurred during the combat, which was a component of Lee's first invasion of the North. Lee's army was repelled by the Union soldiers, who also stopped them from entering further Union territory.

There are a number of important sites and attractions on the battlefield. One of the most recognized buildings on the battlefield is the Dunker Church, a simple white church that survives as a tribute to the conflict. The Sunken Road, also called "Bloody Lane," is a submerged agricultural road that served as the focal point of the battle's fiercest combat.

The park provides visitors with several opportunities to explore and learn about the conflict. There are guided tours, interpretive activities, and a visitor center with artifacts that provide background on the conflict and information. The battlefield has a variety of hiking routes that visitors may use to explore the surroundings and try to picture what could have happened there.

The Antietam National Battlefield serves as a place of meditation and recollection in addition to being an important historical monument. It reminds us of the enormous sacrifices made during the Civil War and its lasting effects on the country. The park draws tourists who are interested in learning about and appreciating the history of the country as well as history buffs and students.

Park National Historic Site of Harpers Ferry

At the meeting of the Potomac and Shenandoah rivers at Harpers Ferry, West Virginia, is where you'll find Harpers Ferry National Historical Park. The town's history, which was important to the formation of the United States, especially in the 19th century, is preserved and explained via the park.

The historical importance of Harpers Ferry spans a number of eras. It was the scene of John Brown's raid in 1859, which is seen as a forerunner to the American Civil War since it heightened tensions between the North and South. Abolitionist John Brown and a handful of supporters planned the attack in an effort to take the Harpers Ferry government armory and spark a slave uprising.

The park also honors its contribution to the American Civil War. It was a location of several conflicts and often changed control between

Union and Confederate armies. Despite the town's considerable wartime destruction, many of its historic structures have been conserved and may still be seen today.

In addition to its involvement in the American Civil War, Harpers Ferry was crucial to the nation's industrial growth. The Harpers Ferry Armory, a government institution that manufactured firearms for the American military, was situated there. The park's displays and interpretive activities highlight the heritage of the armory, a significant hub of industry.

Visitors at Harpers Ferry National Historical Park may stroll along picturesque trails, see the old town, and check out several museums and exhibitions. The park provides insights into the town's rich past via guided tours, living history presentations, and ranger-led events. The John Brown Museum, the Harpers Ferry Armory, and the spectacular vistas that provide panoramic views of the surroundings are among of the park's most well-known attractions.

In addition to being a popular site for history buffs, Harpers Ferry National Historical Park is also a stunning natural setting. In the park, which is a part of the Chesapeake and Ohio Canal National Historical Park, visitors may go hiking, camping, and river rafting.

The whole combination of history, scenic beauty, and recreational options offered by Harpers Ferry National Historical Park is distinctive. It gives tourists an opportunity to learn more about the pivotal moments that molded the country and to take in the town's lovely location at the confluence of two rivers.

Park at Catoctin Mountain

In Frederick County, Maryland, close to the town of Thurmont, there lies a beautiful national park called Catoctin Mountain Park. The

Catoctin Mountain range's eastern slopes are home to the park, which spans more than 5,000 acres of gently sloping hills, woodlands, and streams.

The National Park Service, which oversees the park, provides visitors with a range of outdoor recreational experiences and chances to explore nature. The serene beauty, varied ecosystems, and profusion of species in Catoctin Mountain Park are well-known.

The well-known Cunningham Falls, the biggest cascading waterfall in Maryland, is one of the park's features. The falls are accessible by foot through the park's paths, where visitors may also take in the stunning scenery. There are several additional beautiful routes in the park that meander through forests and provide possibilities for hiking, nature hikes, and birding.

The history of Catoctin Mountain Park is very extensive. The park served as the location of

Camp Misty Mount, a Works Progress Administration (WPA) project in the 1930s. For federal workers and their families, the camp was created as a place of relaxation. Visitors may tour cottages and a stone lodge, two early camp buildings that are still preserved in the park today.

Catoctin Mountain Park is renowned for housing Camp David, the presidential retreat, in addition to its natural and historical attractions. Since Franklin D. Roosevelt's presidency, Camp David, which is located inside the park, has been used by American presidents as a private retreat. Although the area around Camp David is off-limits to the general public, the park offers a chance to see the surroundings that many presidents and international leaders have gotten to enjoy.

The different facilities and services available to visitors in Catoctin Mountain Park are numerous. Visitors may find maps, facts, and displays about the park's natural and cultural heritage at the visitor center, campsites, and picnic spots.

Catoctin Mountain Park provides a picturesque and varied experience for visitors of all ages, whether they are searching for outdoor activity, serene natural settings, or a peek into history.

Saint Mary's City in the past

Along the banks of the St. Mary's River in St. Mary's County, Maryland, sits Historic St. Mary's City, a living history museum and archaeological site. It is a reconstruction of the original Maryland colony's capital, which was founded in 1634 by English colonists as their fourth sustained settlement in North America.

The early colonial era of Maryland's history is intended to be recreated and interpreted at the St.

Mary's City historic site. Through rebuilt houses, gardens, and costumed interpreters, it gives visitors an insight into everyday life in the 17th century. The website is renowned for its historical accuracy and commitment to providing an in-depth look into the past.

The restored State House, which functioned as the epicenter of colonial governance and was the site of significant legislative proceedings, is open to visitors visiting Historic St. Mary's City. The structure sheds light on the political and social circumstances of the early colony. The adjacent Print House exhibits early printed works and demonstrates the printing process in the 17th century.

Another noteworthy aspect of the location is the Godiah Spray Tobacco Plantation. With historically accurate structures and functioning gardens, this plantation serves as a representation of the early colonists' agricultural methods and way of life. Visitors may find information about growing tobacco, doing domestic tasks, and living in slavery or freedom during that time.

Visitors may feel what it was like to traverse the Atlantic during the early days of colonialism by boarding the Maryland Dove, a model of a 17th-century sailing ship that is parked next to the museum. Visitors are given the opportunity to tour the ship's decks and learn about the difficulties of nautical navigation at the period via an immersive and informative experience.

Historic St. Mary's City holds several events, reenactments, and educational activities all through the year that bring the colonial era to life. Visitors may engage with costumed interpreters who recreate the life of the early settlers, see live demonstrations, and take part in practical activities.

The St. Mary's City Archaeological Research and Collections Facility is located on the site, where continuing archaeological studies are carried out to find and examine the ruins of the old village. The information gained from these digs advances our knowledge of Maryland's colonial past and the current study being done on it.

A special chance to go back in time and learn more about Maryland's early colonial era is offered by Historic St. Mary's City. It provides visitors with a range of engaging interactive activities, historically accurate reconstructions, and archaeological research.

National Historic Site of Thomas Stone

The home and estate of Thomas Stone, a well-known Founding Father of the United States, are preserved at the Thomas Stone National Historic Site in Charles County, Maryland. Thomas Stone contributed significantly to forming the early history of the country as one of the Declaration of Independence's signatories.

Thomas Stone's former home, Haberdeventure, an 18th-century plantation mansion, is included in the historic site. Visitors may get a look into Thomas Stone and his family's lives and times by visiting the immaculately preserved mansion, which has been scrupulously restored to its original appearance.

Visitors at Thomas Stone National Historic Site may wander the grounds and receive guided tours of the plantation home. Insights on Thomas Stone's contributions to the Revolutionary War, his part in writing the Declaration of Independence, and his function in the early years of the United States are provided via the guided tours.

There is also a visitor center at the location where people may find out more about Thomas Stone's life and the historical setting in which it occurred. A fuller knowledge of the importance of the site and the overall history of the United States during the Revolutionary Era may be gained through the exhibits, displays, and interactive presentations.

The Thomas Stone National Historic Site is significant historically and provides chances for outdoor leisure. Walking paths on the property go through the picturesque surroundings of Haberdeventure. These pathways provide visitors the chance to discover the region's natural beauties and take in the tranquil atmosphere of the historic site.

The Thomas Stone National Historic Site honors Thomas Stone's services to the country and gives visitors an opportunity to engage with American history from the country's early years. Visitors may learn about the life of a Founding Father and have a greater understanding of the ideas and sacrifices that molded the country's history in this peaceful and informative environment.

Chapter 8

Nature Adventures in Maryland

Lake Deep Creek

The biggest freshwater lake in the American state of Maryland is called Deep Creek Lake. It is situated in Garrett County, which is in the state's western region. Listed below are some facts regarding Deep Creek Lake:

1. Location: Deep Creek Lake may be found in Maryland's Allegheny Mountains, about 8 miles (13 kilometers) south of Oakland.

2. Size: The lake has a coastline that runs for roughly 69 miles (111 kilometers) and has an

approximate size of 3,900 acres (1,600 hectares). It may be as deep as 23 meters or 75 feet.

3. Construction of the Deep Creek Dam on Deep Creek, a Youghiogheny River tributary, led to the formation of Deep Creek Lake in 1925. The dam was constructed to provide hydroelectric electricity.

4. Recreation: Deep Creek Lake is a well-liked vacation spot that provides a variety of activities. The lake is a popular place for boating, fishing, swimming, water skiing, kayaking, and paddleboarding. The lake is renowned for providing good fishing possibilities for species including trout, walleye, yellow perch, trout, and smallmouth and largemouth bass.

5. Deep Creek Lake State Park is a state park that surrounds the lake and provides visitors with a range of services and amenities. The park has campgrounds, picnic spots, walking paths, a swimming beach, and a boat ramp. Outdoor aficionados and nature lovers will enjoy it here.

6. Deep Creek Lake is another well-liked wintertime vacation spot. Visitors may do skiing, snowboarding, snow tubing, and snowmobiling in the region because of the typical snowfall. Near the lake, Wisp Resort has downhill skiing and snowboarding amenities.

7. Area: The Deep Creek Lake region is renowned for its stunning scenery and unspoiled natural beauty. It is bordered by wooded hills, and in the autumn, the foliage's shifting hues make it a well-liked location for leaf-peeping.

8. Tourism: Throughout the year, the lake draws a large number of visitors from Maryland and its adjacent states. Visitors that travel to the lake and its surrounds may stay in a variety of lodging options, including resorts, cottages, and vacation rentals.

Overall, Deep Creek Lake is a well-liked location for outdoor enthusiasts, nature lovers, and those looking for a quiet break in Maryland since it provides a stunning natural environment and a variety of recreational activities.

State Park of Patapsco Valley

In the heart of Maryland, United States, Patapsco Valley State Park is a sizable public leisure area situated beside the Patapsco River. Here are some details on Patapsco Valley State Park:

1. Patapsco Valley State Park spans a 32-mile (51-kilometer) section of the Patapsco River and is located in the counties of Howard and Baltimore. It is about 10 miles (16 kilometers) from downtown and situated just southwest of Baltimore.

2. One of Maryland's biggest state parks, the park is approximately 16,000 acres (6,475 hectares) in size. It has a variety of topographies,

such as woods, valleys, meadows, and historical monuments.

3. History: The park has a long, illustrious history that dates to the early nineteenth century. In the past, the region was home to industries and mill towns that made use of the river's power for production. The park still contains the ruins of ancient mills and other historical buildings, providing an insight into its industrial history.

4. Visitors may engage in a variety of recreational activities at Patapsco Valley State Park. The park's extensive network of hiking and bike paths offers chances for outdoor exploration and adventure. Within the park, other well-liked activities include bird viewing, horseback riding, camping, and fishing.

5. Swinging Bridges: The park's abundance of swinging bridges is one of its distinctive attractions. Visitors may cross the river on these suspension bridges at different locations, and

they also provide beautiful views of the surroundings.

6. Water Sports: The Patapsco River provides chances for water sports including tubing, canoeing, and kayaking. There are places set out for swimming and wading.

7. Wildlife and Natural Beauty: A wide variety of plant and animal species call the park home. While walking the park's pathways, visitors could run with white-tailed deer, foxes, raccoons, and numerous bird species. For outdoor enthusiasts and environment lovers, the surroundings provide gorgeous waterfalls, peaceful streams, and thick woods as a wonderful background.

8. Historic Sites: Patapsco Valley State Park is home to a number of interesting historic sites. A beautiful stone bridge that previously supported the Baltimore and Ohio Railroad is known as the Thomas Viaduct and is a National Historic Landmark. Old mill villages and dam ruins are

also present, highlighting the park's industrial past.

In addition to offering a variety of outdoor activities, Patapsco Valley State Park is also significant historically. The park offers a tranquil and enjoyable respite close to the busy city of Baltimore, whether you're wanting to walk, cycle, visit historical monuments, or just appreciate nature.

Park at Cunningham Falls

A beautiful state park called Cunningham Falls State Park may be found in Frederick County, Maryland's Catoctin Mountains. Listed below are some details on Cunningham Falls State Park:

1. Location: Cunningham Falls State Park is about 20 miles (32 kilometers) north of

Frederick, in the vicinity of Thurmont, Maryland. Within the Catoctin Mountain range, it has an area of around 6,000 acres (2,428 hectares).

2. Cunningham Falls: Cunningham Falls, Maryland's biggest cascading waterfall, inspired the park's name. With a height of around 78 feet (24 meters), the falls are a noticeable natural feature in the park. Visitors may take in beautiful views of the falls and the nearby forest.

3. Outdoor Recreational Activities: Visitors may engage in a range of outdoor recreational activities at Cunningham Falls State Park. With more than 30 miles (48 kilometers) of trails accessible, hiking is especially well-liked. The varied complexity of the routes offers opportunities for hikers of all abilities. Mountain biking and equestrian riding have their own pathways in the park.

4. Hunting and fishing are both allowed in certain park areas during particular seasons as

long as you abide by the rules set out by the Maryland Department of Natural Resources. Hunting Creek Lake, Cunningham Falls Lake, and the neighboring Big Hunting Creek are the three primary bodies of water in the park where fishing is permitted. Anglers may attempt to capture fish including trout, bass, and bluegill.

5. Hunting Creek Lake at Cunningham Falls State Park has been classified as a swimming place. Over the course of the summer, tourists may unwind, tan, and cool off in the water at the sandy beach. Typically, lifeguards are on duty during busy hours.

6. Camping and Picnicking: The park has a number of picnic spots with tables, grills, and shelters so that guests may have outdoor meals and get-togethers. In addition, Cunningham Falls State Park has tent and RV camping facilities. The park has a number of campsites, including those in the William Houck, Manor, and Catoctin Furnace areas.

7. Nature Programs and Interpretive Center: Throughout the year, the park provides a variety of nature programs, led walks, and educational activities. The William Houck Area's visitor center acts as a resource for guests and disseminates knowledge about the natural and cultural heritage of the park.

Outdoor enthusiasts, nature lovers, and families looking for recreational options and scenic views frequent Cunningham Falls State Park. The park provides a tranquil and gorgeous location for tourists to enjoy the great outdoors with its magnificent waterfall, scenic paths, swimming area, and camping amenities.

Great Park Falls

A stunning and historic park called Great Falls Park is situated on the Potomac River in

Virginia, not far from Washington, D.C. The following details about Great Falls Park:

1. Location: In Fairfax County, Virginia, next to the hamlet of Great Falls, Great Falls Park is situated along the Potomac River, some 15 miles (24 kilometers) northwest of the center of Washington, D.C.

2. Natural Attractions: The Great Falls of the Potomac may be seen in all their magnificence from the park. A succession of steep ledges are crossed by the river, resulting in spectacular waterfalls that are awe-inspiring to see for tourists. Outdoor activities are set against a picturesque background of mountainous terrain and precipitous cliffs.

3. Nature and hiking paths are available in Great Falls Park, allowing visitors to experience the region's breathtaking scenery. The River Trail is a well-liked option since it offers beautiful waterfall views and chances to see animals. The park also offers a number of other routes with

varied degrees of difficulty to accommodate different hiking styles.

4. Scenic Overlooks: Throughout the park, there are a number of overlook locations that provide expansive views of the Potomac River and the cascading falls. These vistas provide fantastic picture possibilities and let tourists appreciate the breathtaking beauty of the surroundings.

5. For those who like rock climbing, Great Falls Park is a well-liked site. Climbers of all abilities may find difficult climbs on the cliffs near the Potomac River. It's crucial to remember that climbing is only allowed in specific places and with the appropriate permissions.

6. Picnicking & Picnic sites: The park offers picnic sites where guests may relax and eat in the middle of the landscape. Families and parties may enjoy picnics outside in these locations since they are furnished with grills and picnic tables.

7. Great Falls area contains a visitor center with exhibits highlighting the natural and cultural heritage of the area. Visitors may discover the geological origins of the falls, the history of the local Native Americans, and how the park influenced the growth of the area. Additionally, the visitor center offers educational events and information on park activities.

8. Park visitors of all ages may participate in a variety of ranger-led programs and activities. These events provide insights into the park's value both naturally and culturally via guided walks, discussions, and demonstrations.

Outdoor enthusiasts, nature lovers, and people looking for a quiet getaway from the city often visit Great Falls Park. The park provides a unique experience and an opportunity to get in touch with nature, whether you're interested in hiking, rock climbing, picnicking, or just taking in the stunning majesty of the falls.

State Park of Assateague

On Assateague Island in Maryland and Virginia, there is a coastal park called Assateague State Park. Here are some details on Assateague State Park:

1. Location: Assateague State Park is located on the barrier island of Assateague Island, which is situated in the Atlantic Ocean. Assateague State Park is located on the Maryland half of the island, which is split between Maryland and Virginia.

2. Beaches: The park is renowned for its stunning, sandy shorelines that extend for kilometers. Swimmers, sunbathers, beachcombers, and sandcastle builders may all have fun here. The unspoiled natural beauty of Assateague Island's beaches is what makes them so attractive.

3. Animals: Assateague Island is well-known for its wild horses, sometimes referred to as Chincoteague ponies or Assateague horses. These wild horses are a top draw for tourists and wander freely around the island. It's possible to see these magnificent creatures in the park's natural setting, but it's crucial to preserve your distance and avoid approaching or feeding them.

4. Camping: For guests who want to stay the night on the island, Assateague State Park has camping areas. The campground offers both tent and RV camping spaces, along with conveniences like picnic tables, fire pits, and restrooms. Visitors may explore the distinctive atmosphere of the island and take in the sounds of the ocean by camping on Assateague.

5. Hiking and Nature Trails: Visitors may explore the island's many ecosystems on the park's many hiking and nature trails. The paths provide possibilities for animal and bird viewing, as well as magnificent views of the marshes, dune fields, and woodlands on the

island. A well-liked route in the park is the Life of the Forest Nature route.

6. Kayaking and canoeing: Assateague State Park is a great place to kayak and paddle since it offers access to the island's adjacent coastal waters. Paddling around the serene coves and canals allows visitors to take in the tranquility of the setting and the possibility of seeing animals.

7. Assateague Island is a sanctuary for birdwatchers as many migrating bird species stop there as a resting place. Numerous species of birds are drawn to the island's diverse ecosystems, which include salt marshes, forests, and beaches, throughout the year. During their stay, guests may see shorebirds, ducks, raptors, and other species.

8. informative Programs: The park provides educational activities and informative programs for visitors of all ages. These programs cover a range of subjects, including the animals, environment, and cultural history of the island.

They could consist of seminars, tours, and hands-on exhibitions.

With its stunning beaches, wild horses, and varied natural habitats, Assateague State Park offers a distinctive coastal experience. The park provides a spectacular and engrossing outdoor experience on the beaches of the Atlantic Ocean, whether you're interested in camping, beach activities, animal observation, or exploring the island's paths.

Chapter 9

Cultural Experiences in Maryland

Maryland Renaissance Festival

Every year in late summer and early autumn, Crownsville, Maryland, hosts the Maryland Renaissance Festival. One of the biggest and most well-liked Renaissance events in the country is this one. The event honors English Renaissance culture, music, art, and entertainment from the sixteenth century.

Visitors may immerse themselves in a reconstructed English hamlet during the event, replete with period-style structures, attire, and activities. The residents of the hamlet are actors and entertainers who play nobility, peasants, knights, and jesters from the Renaissance period.

The Maryland Renaissance Festival offers a variety of attractions and events for guests to enjoy. These consist of live performances by musicians, dancers, comedians, and jousting teams, as well as live comedy acts. Additionally, visitors may browse artist booths offering a variety of handcrafted goods including jewelry, apparel, and accessories. Traditional Renaissance cuisine including turkey legs, mead, and ale are available as food and beverage alternatives.

The Maryland Renaissance Festival's jousting contests, where knights in full armor compete in exciting matches on horseback, are one of the festival's highlights. The festival often holds themed weekends, like Pirate Weekend or Celtic Celebration, that give the whole experience a distinctive flavor.

The information supplied here is based on the knowledge cutoff of September 2021, thus it's vital to keep in mind that some specifics concerning the event may have altered since then. For the most recent details on dates, costs, and attractions, it is always a good idea to visit the Maryland Renaissance Festival's official website or get in touch with the festival's organizers.

Sites of African American Heritage

Historic places that honor the accomplishments and experiences of African Americans throughout history are known as African American heritage sites. These websites often feature African Americans' hardships, triumphs, and cultural heritage, bringing light on their experiences and encouraging understanding and respect of their contributions to society. Here are a few significant African American heritage locations in the US:

1. The Smithsonian Institution's National Museum of African American History and Culture is located in Washington, D.C., and it has exhibits on the history, culture, and accomplishments of African Americans. It has a sizable collection of artifacts, displays, and hands-on activities that look at many facets of African American history.

2. King, Martin Luther Jr. In Atlanta, Georgia, there is a national historic site that houses Dr. Martin Luther King Jr.'s boyhood home as well as the Ebenezer Baptist Church where he gave sermons. The King Center, which houses his grave and a museum devoted to his life and legacy, is another attraction of the location.

3. The National Underground Railroad Freedom Center (Cincinnati, Ohio) is a museum that studies the history of the Underground Railroad, a system of covert paths and safe houses that

enslaved African Americans used to escape to free states and Canada. The museum explores contemporary human rights concerns as well as the tales of liberation fighters and abolitionists.

4. The Birmingham Civil Rights Institute is a museum that documents the difficulties and victories of the civil rights movement in Birmingham and across the United States. It is located in Birmingham, Alabama. Segregation, the struggle for voting rights, and the accomplishments of civil rights leaders are just a few of the issues covered in the displays.

5. Whitney Plantation (Wallace, Louisiana): The Whitney Plantation is a former sugar plantation that has been converted into a museum with a specialization on the lives and experiences of slaves. In order to inform tourists about the brutal reality of slavery, it conducts guided tours that give historical background and human anecdotes.

6. An estimated 15,000 free and enslaved Africans were buried here during the late 17th and early 18th centuries, according to estimates made at the time of the site's discovery in the 1990s. The monument has a memorial and visitor center that honor the people buried there and examine their contributions to the growth of New York City.

These are just a few instances of African American heritage locations found all around the country. There are countless additional locations that honor the rich history and tradition of African Americans in various parts of the nation, including regional museums, historic sites, and cultural hubs.

The National Historic Site of Frederick Douglass

Washington, DC is home to the Frederick Douglass National Historic Site. It pays homage to the life and contributions of Frederick Douglass, a well-known abolitionist, author, and statesman of African American descent. On the property stands Douglass's previous home, Cedar Hill, where he resided from 1877 until his death in 1895.

The historic mansion, which has been restored to resemble its look during Douglass's time, is available for guided tours for visitors to the Frederick Douglass National Historic Site. Insights into Douglass's life, including his runaway from slavery, his work as an abolitionist and orator, and his contributions to the civil rights movement, are given throughout the tour.

The location has a tourist center with displays on Douglass's life, writings, and effect in addition to the home. The exhibitions emphasize his contributions to the abolitionist cause and his support of women's and African American's equal rights. Visitors may delve further into Douglass' achievements and the social and political environment of his day by seeing artifacts, images, and interactive exhibits.

The Frederick Douglass National Historic Site also provides educational activities, gatherings, and special talks that explore many facets of Douglass's activism and life. These workshops aim to spark discussion and advance a better understanding of the continuing fight for justice and equality.

For the most up-to-date information on visiting hours, tour availability, and any special events or displays, it is advised to consult the official website or get in touch with the Frederick Douglass National Historic Site directly.

Museum of Reginald F. Lewis

Baltimore, Maryland is the home of the Reginald F. Lewis Museum of Maryland African American History & Culture. It bears Reginald F. Lewis' name, a well-known businessman and philanthropist of African American descent. The goal of the museum is to preserve, record, and present the history and culture of African Americans in Maryland.

Numerous exhibitions in the Reginald F. Lewis Museum address various facets of African American history, art, and culture. African diaspora, the fight for civil rights, African American contributions to the arts, music, sports, and other issues are just a few of the many subjects covered by the displays. The African American experience in Maryland and its larger relevance may be better understood by visitors via artifacts, pictures, works of art, and multimedia displays.

The museum also provides lectures, seminars, and educational activities that give chances for learning, conversation, and community involvement. These programs often center on issues of social justice, cultural heritage, and African American history.

The Reginald F. Lewis Museum also presents unique concerts, exhibits, and events that celebrate the achievements of African American intellectuals, musicians, and artists. In addition to creating venues for cultural expression and appreciation, these activities strive to showcase African American culture.

Check the Reginald F. Lewis Museum's official website for the most recent details on hours of operation, admission costs, available exhibits, and any COVID-19 safety precautions if you want to attend.

National Great Blacks Museum of Wax Figures

Baltimore, Maryland is where the National Great Blacks In Wax Museum is situated. It's a special museum that emphasizes the historical accomplishments and contributions of African Americans. The museum teaches visitors about the tales and experiences of African Americans via life-size wax models, historical relics, and immersive exhibitions.

The National Great Blacks In Wax Museum's displays include famous people from several historical eras. African civilizations, the transatlantic slave trade, the civil rights struggle, and modern African American leaders are among the topics covered in the displays available to visitors. The museum's mission is to provide an in-depth and compelling history of African Americans, showcasing both well-known people and unsung heroes.

The National Great Blacks In Wax Museum is distinguished by its employment of realistic wax models to represent historical personalities. This adds a feeling of realism and makes the experience for visitors more immersive. These figurines are expertly constructed to mimic the look and mannerisms of the people they portray.

The museum provides educational events and seminars that encourage learning and conversation about African American history and culture in addition to the exhibits. Both kids and adults may benefit from the programs' chances for experiential and participatory learning.

It is advised to check the National Great Blacks In Wax Museum's official website for the most recent details on their hours of operation, entrance costs, and any special exhibitions or events before making travel arrangements. By doing this, you can be confident that the information you have for your visit is up to date and pertinent.

Visiting Galleries and Museums

Baltimore, Maryland is home to the renowned Baltimore Museum of Art (BMA). It is renowned across the world for its huge collection of artwork from many eras and genres. The Baltimore Museum of Art's salient features are as follows:

- Collection: The British Museum has an extraordinary collection of about 95,000 pieces of art, which includes ornamental arts, prints, drawings, photos, and sculptures. The collection includes artwork from many different eras, including both ancient and modern pieces.

- Highlights: Famous painters including Henri Matisse, Pablo Picasso, Vincent van Gogh, Andy Warhol, Georgia O'Keeffe, and Jackson Pollock have pieces in the museum's collection.

Important works include "Blue Nude II" by Matisse, "The Olive Trees" by van Gogh, and "Divas" by Warhol.

- Contemporary Art: The BMA places a lot of emphasis on this genre and has acquired substantial pieces from it. Its collection of contemporary artworks, which represents the cutting-edge and varied creative practices of the present, comprises works from all around the globe.

- The Cone Collection: The Cone Collection is one of the most well-known components in the BMA's collection. Two Baltimore sisters named Claribel and Etta Cone gathered a spectacular collection of contemporary art, which included a sizable number of Matisse pieces. One of the best collections of early 20th-century European art in the world is said to be the Cone Collection.

- Special exhibits: The BMA presents transient exhibits that examine a range of subjects, artists, and artistic trends in addition to its permanent collection. Loans from other museums and private collections are often included in these displays, giving viewers a dynamic and constantly-changing experience.

- Education and Programs: To engage visitors of all ages and backgrounds, the BMA provides a variety of educational programs, including lectures, seminars, and guided tours. These initiatives seek to improve people's knowledge of and appreciation for art.

- Building and Amenities: The BMA is located in a historic structure that is surrounded by lovely park-like scenery. There are many galleries, a sculpture garden, a library, a café, and a museum store inside the establishment.

One may get fully immersed in a vast and varied collection of art by visiting the Baltimore Museum of Art. The BMA provides a rich and fulfilling experience for everyone, whether you are an enthusiastic scholar, a casual tourist, or an art aficionado.

Baltimore Museum of Art

The Walters Art Museum is a well-known cultural institution with an extraordinary collection of artwork from many different countries and time periods. It is situated in Baltimore, Maryland. The Walters Art Museum's salient characteristics are as follows:

- Collection: The museum's collection totals about 36,000 items, comprising works of art from the ancient worlds of Egypt, Greece, and Rome, medieval Europe, masterpieces from the Renaissance and Baroque periods, as well as Asian, Islamic, and decorative arts. The range and excellence of the collection are well known.

- Highlights: The Walters Art Museum is home to several important pieces of art. A few notable works include Hieronymus Bosch's "The Last Judgment" from the 16th century, Catherine of

Cleves' illuminated "Book of Hours," from the 15th century, and the Lady Sha-Amun-em-su mummy from ancient Egypt.

- Ancient Art: Sculptures, jewelry, ceramics, and other objects from earlier civilizations are included in the museum's collection of ancient art. Through these extraordinary items, visitors may learn about the art and culture of ancient Egypt, Greece, Rome, and the Near East.

- Renaissance and Baroque Art: The Walters Art Museum is home to a sizable collection of Renaissance and Baroque artworks, including pieces by famous European painters including Sandro Botticelli, Peter Paul Rubens, and Rembrandt van Rijn. The collection includes decorative arts, sculptures, and paintings from this pivotal time in art history.

- Asian Art: The museum's collection of Asian art includes pieces from China, Japan, Korea, and other countries. The many creative traditions of different civilizations are shown via the pottery, paintings, calligraphy, sculptures, and textiles that are part of it.

Islamic art is well represented in the Walters Art Museum's impressive collection, which spans ages and geographical areas. Exquisite carpets, pottery, metalwork, manuscripts, and other items that showcase the richness and beauty of Islamic aesthetic traditions are available for visitors to examine.

- Educational Programs: The Walters Art Museum provides a range of educational activities, like as tours, talks, seminars, and family events. These initiatives seek to enrich the knowledge and enjoyment of art and culture in visitors of all ages.

- Facilities: The museum is situated in a landmark structure in Baltimore's Mount Vernon district. The building has a number of galleries, a lab for conservation, a café, and a museum store.

Visitors may study and enjoy pieces of art from all centuries and civilizations at the Walters Art Museum, which is a veritable gold mine of art and culture. The museum provides a thorough and educational experience, regardless of your particular interest in ancient art, Renaissance masterpieces, Asian customs, or Islamic cultural legacy.

Walters Art Gallery

The Walters Art Museum is a well-known cultural institution with an extraordinary collection of artwork from many different countries and time periods. It is situated in Baltimore, Maryland. The Walters Art Museum's salient characteristics are as follows:

- Collection: The museum's collection totals about 36,000 items, comprising works of art from the ancient worlds of Egypt, Greece, and Rome, medieval Europe, masterpieces from the

Renaissance and Baroque periods, as well as Asian, Islamic, and decorative arts. The range and excellence of the collection are well known.

- Highlights: The Walters Art Museum is home to several important pieces of art. A few notable works include Hieronymus Bosch's "The Last Judgment" from the 16th century, Catherine of Cleves' illuminated "Book of Hours," from the 15th century, and the Lady Sha-Amun-em-su mummy from ancient Egypt.

- Ancient Art: Sculptures, jewelry, ceramics, and other objects from earlier civilizations are included in the museum's collection of ancient art. Through these extraordinary items, visitors may learn about the art and culture of ancient Egypt, Greece, Rome, and the Near East.

- Renaissance and Baroque Art: The Walters Art Museum is home to a sizable collection of Renaissance and Baroque artworks, including pieces by famous European painters including Sandro Botticelli, Peter Paul Rubens, and

Rembrandt van Rijn. The collection includes decorative arts, sculptures, and paintings from this pivotal time in art history.

- Asian Art: The museum's collection of Asian art includes pieces from China, Japan, Korea, and other countries. The many creative traditions of different civilizations are shown via the pottery, paintings, calligraphy, sculptures, and textiles that are part of it.

Islamic art is well represented in the Walters Art Museum's impressive collection, which spans ages and geographical areas. Exquisite carpets, pottery, metalwork, manuscripts, and other items that showcase the richness and beauty of Islamic aesthetic traditions are available for visitors to examine.

- Educational Programs: The Walters Art Museum provides a range of educational activities, like as tours, talks, seminars, and family events. These initiatives seek to enrich the knowledge and enjoyment of art and culture in visitors of all ages.

- Facilities: The museum is situated in a landmark structure in Baltimore's Mount Vernon district. The building has a number of galleries, a lab for conservation, a café, and a museum store.

Visitors may study and enjoy pieces of art from all centuries and civilizations at the Walters Art Museum, which is a veritable gold mine of art and culture. The museum provides a thorough and educational experience, regardless of your particular interest in ancient art, Renaissance masterpieces, Asian customs, or Islamic cultural legacy.

National Museum of Health and Medicine

The National Museum of Health and Medicine (NMHM) is a museum devoted to preserving and exhibiting the history of health and medical achievements. It is situated in Silver Spring, Maryland, just outside of Washington, D.C. Several important facts regarding the National Museum of Health and Medicine are provided below:

- History and Purpose: The Army Medical Museum, which is now known as the National Museum of Health and Medicine, was founded during the American Civil War with the aim of recording medical developments and conserving anatomical specimens for study and instruction. The collection, preservation, and interpretation of items associated with health, medicine, and the medical sciences is the current focus of the museum.

- Collections: There are nearly 25 million items in the museum's collection, including anatomical specimens, medical devices, pictures, records, and other historical relics. The collection includes articles on a variety of subjects, such as pathology, surgery, forensic medicine, and medical research.

- displays: The NMHM has a number of displays that examine the development of medicine and its social implications. Displays of preserved human organs and tissues, medical equipment and tools, interactive multimedia presentations, and old photos and papers are a few examples of exhibits.

- Notable Artifacts: The museum is home to a number of important artifacts, including, among others, the bullet that killed President Abraham Lincoln, samples gathered during the Spanish Flu outbreak, and the bones of a Confederate soldier with a bullet implanted in it.

- Education and Outreach: For students, researchers, and the general public, the National Museum of Health and Medicine provides educational programs, seminars, and lectures. These initiatives seek to increase knowledge of medical progress, research, and history.

- Walter Reed Army Institute of Research: The Walter Reed Army Institute of Research, which carries out biomedical research and aids military medical missions, is closely related to the museum. The museum and the institution often work together on exhibits and research initiatives.

- Information for Visitors: The NMHM is accessible to everyone and welcomes visitors of all ages. The museum provides educational events, guided tours, and access to its holdings for scholarly study.

The National Museum of Health and Medicine offers a distinctive viewpoint on the development of healthcare and the history of medicine. It is a fascinating location for anyone interested in medical history, anatomy, and the development of healthcare practices since it provides a fascinating insight into the area of medical research and its effects on society.

The Maryland Wine Region

The state of Maryland has a number of wine-producing areas, which together make up the state's wine country. These areas are renowned for producing a range of wines, including classic European-style wines and distinctive regional varieties. Here are some essential facts regarding Maryland's wine region:

1. Eastern Shore: Maryland's eastern shore is home to the Eastern Shore area, which provides a gorgeous backdrop for wineries and vineyards. Due to its close proximity to the Chesapeake Bay, the area has a climate that is ideal for growing grapes. Chardonnay, Cabernet Sauvignon, and Merlot are three common grape varietals cultivated in this region.

2. Piedmont Plateau: The undulating hills and rich soils of the Piedmont Plateau area in central Maryland are ideal for growing grapes.

Award-winning red wines like Cabernet Franc and Petit Verdot, as well as Chardonnay and Sauvignon Blanc, are made in this region.

3. Patapsco Valley: The Patapsco Valley area, close to Baltimore, is distinguished for its picturesque vistas and historic charm. The vineyards in this area benefit from the surrounding Chesapeake Bay's moderating effect, which creates a perfect microclimate for grape cultivation. Chardonnay, Pinot Gris, and Cabernet Sauvignon are just a few of the wines that are produced in this area.

4. Catoctin Mountain: Due to its greater height, the Catoctin Mountain area in western Maryland provides a milder temperature. The vines in this area profit from the steep topography, producing wines with unique qualities. The grapes Cabernet Franc, Chambourcin, and Vidal Blanc are widely farmed in this area.

5. One of the most well-known wineries in Maryland is Linganore Winecellars, which is

located in the Catoctin Mountain area. It provides both dry and sweet wines in a variety of flavors. The vineyard offers festivals and events all through the year, giving guests the chance to experience wine tastings, live music, and regional cuisine.

6. Another well-known winery in Maryland is Black Ankle Vineyards, which is situated on the Piedmont Plateau. It emphasizes environmentally friendly methods and makes premium wines, such as Chardonnay and Bordeaux-style blends. Visitors may sample the outstanding wines at the vineyard via tours and tastings.

7. Wine Trails: The Maryland wine region is also home to a number of wine trails that highlight several wineries in a particular area. Visitors have the chance to tour several vineyards and take in the natural beauty of the surroundings on these trails, such the Patuxent Wine Trail and the Chesapeake Wine Trail.

Wine lovers may experience Maryland's expanding wine industry, sample a range of wines, and take in the picturesque vineyard landscapes by traveling to the state's wine region. Maryland's wine districts provide a varied range to suit your palette, whether you favor red, white, or rosé wines.

Ocean City Boardwalk

In Ocean City, Maryland, there is a well-known tourist destination called the Ocean City Boardwalk. The boardwalk provides a bustling and energetic environment with a variety of entertainment choices, shops, restaurants, and attractions along its three-mile length along the Atlantic Ocean. Here are some significant specifics of the Ocean City Boardwalk:

1. Attractions and Rides: Several amusement parks, including Trimper's Rides and Jolly Roger

at the Pier, are located along the boardwalk. These amusement parks provide fun for guests of all ages with a variety of rides and attractions including roller coasters, Ferris wheels, bumper cars, and traditional carnival games.

2. Dining and Snacks: There are a ton of dining establishments on the boardwalk, from casual diners to seafood restaurants and food carts. In addition to the state's well-known blue crabs, visitors may eat pizza, ice cream, funnel cakes, saltwater taffy, fresh seafood, and other traditional boardwalk foods.

3. stores and Boutiques: There are many different stores and boutiques along the boardwalk, each of which sells a wide range of goods. To remember their journey to Ocean City, tourists may buy beachwear, trinkets, jewelry, original artwork, surfboards, and presents that are only available there.

4. Entertainment: Street performers, magicians, live music shows, and other shows are often held

on the boardwalk. While wandering down the boardwalk, visitors may take in free concerts, magic performances, and other types of live entertainment.

5. The Ocean City Boardwalk is a well-liked location for morning strolls and bike excursions. Rental bicycles are available at many points along the boardwalk, enabling guests to take in the beautiful beach views while being active.

6. Beach Access: The boardwalk offers easy access to Ocean City's sandy beaches. Before or after viewing the boardwalk activities, visitors may relax on the beach, go swimming in the water, or just enjoy the sunshine.

7. Festivals & Events: The Ocean City Boardwalk organizes several festivals and events every year. These events include Sunfest, Springfest, OC Air Show, and Beach Lights during the holiday season. The boardwalk experience is further enhanced by these events in terms of excitement and entertainment.

The Ocean City Boardwalk is a must-visit location for travelers in Maryland because of its lively and active environment. The Ocean City Boardwalk has something for everyone, whether you're looking for exhilarating rides, delectable cuisine, one-of-a-kind shopping opportunities, or just a quiet stroll along the shore.

Chapter 10

Practical Tips and Safety Information

Health and Safety Recommendations

Following are some basic health and security recommendations for visitors to Maryland:

1. COVID-19 Safety Measures: Keep up with Maryland's most recent COVID-19 regulations and requirements. Before your journey, check for any quarantine or travel warnings.

2. Vaccination: If you are qualified and haven't had a COVID-19 shot, think about obtaining one

before going abroad. A powerful method of defending both yourself and others is vaccination.

3. Face Masks: Comply with any regulations or mandates that may be in place. When social distance cannot be maintained, use a mask in busy outdoor areas, public places indoors, and such situations.

4. Physically remove yourself from those who aren't family members by keeping a distance of at least 6 feet (2 meters).

5. Hand hygiene: Consistently wash your hands with warm water and soap for at least 20 seconds. Use hand sanitizer containing at least 60% alcohol if soap and water are not available.

6. Limit Close Contact: Keep distance from those who are unwell or exhibiting signs of sickness.

7. Stay at Home if Ill: If you have any signs of an illness, such as a fever, cough, or breathing problems, stay at home and get help from a doctor.

8. Adhere to any travel advice or recommendations published by the CDC or regional health authorities. Information on necessary tests, suggested quarantines, and other travel-related limitations are included.

9. Research Local Services: Become acquainted with the area's COVID-19 testing locations, local hospitals, and emergency phone numbers.

10. Stay Current: Keep up with the most recent rules and changes by often visiting reputable websites like the CDC and the Maryland Department of Health.

Keep in mind that these suggestions are subject to modification, so it's essential to keep up to date on them both before and during your trip.

Exchange of money and currencies

The United States Dollar (USD) is the main currency utilized in Maryland when it comes to money and currency exchange. Following are some key considerations:

1. Currency: The United States Dollar (USD) is the nation's legal currency. Make sure you arrive with enough USD currency to cover your immediate requirements.

2. Cash and Cards: In Maryland, particularly in metropolitan areas and popular tourist locations, major credit and debit cards are frequently accepted. For smaller businesses or locations that may not take credit cards, it's a good idea to have some cash on hand.

3. Currency Exchange: Banks, currency exchange offices, and certain hotels all allow

you to convert foreign cash for USD. To receive the greatest deal, it is necessary to compare exchange rates and costs. There could be currency exchange facilities at certain international airports, but the prices might not be as good.

4. There are several automated teller machines (ATMs) throughout Maryland. You are able to use your debit or credit card to withdraw money in USD via them. Be cautious of any possible fees or international transaction costs that your bank may apply, however.

5. Traveler's checks: These days, fewer people use them, so it could be hard to locate locations that take them. Carrying cash or using a debit or credit card is often more practical.

6. Foreign Currency Acceptance: Although some bigger businesses may take foreign money, it is often advised to utilize US dollars when doing business in Maryland. Local sellers and smaller companies may not take foreign cash.

7. Exchange Rates: Exchange rates vary based on where you exchange your money and are subject to daily fluctuations. Before exchanging money, it's a good idea to check the current rates to be sure you're receiving a fair price.

8. Security: Be careful and safeguard any cash you bring. In general, it is better to make bigger purchases using credit or debit cards and to maintain a modest amount of cash on hand for smaller ones.

To prevent any possible problems with card transactions, don't forget to let your bank or credit card provider know about your vacation intentions. Having a variety of payment options is also a smart idea so you have options in case of any unanticipated occurrences.

Access to the Internet and communication

There are several ways to keep connected in Maryland when it comes to communication and internet connection. The following are some crucial considerations:

1. Mobile Networks: Major mobile network providers including AT&T, Verizon, T-Mobile, and Sprint provide dependable service throughout Maryland. Make sure your mobile device is compatible with the required network, or if you have an unlocked phone, think about buying a local SIM card.

2. Roaming Fees: Inquire about international roaming fees from your cell service provider if you're going from another nation. Due to the high cost of roaming fees, buying a local SIM card or thinking about utilizing Wi-Fi are often more economical options.

3. Wi-Fi Accessibility: at Maryland, Wi-Fi is often accessible at hotels, coffee shops, dining

establishments, airports, and other public areas. Many establishments provide free Wi-Fi connection, although others could demand payment or have time limits. For information about the Wi-Fi access, contact the business.

4. Internet Cafes: Due to the extensive use of Wi-Fi, internet cafes may not be as common as they previously were. However, bigger cities or popular tourist destinations may still have some internet cafés or business centers.

5. Public Libraries: There is a network of public libraries in Maryland that often provide free internet connection to locals and guests. Ask your local library about its rules about visitors.

6. Virtual Private Networks (VPNs): Think about utilizing a VPN service if you want to browse the internet safely or get around any geographical limitations. Your internet connection may be encrypted with the use of a VPN, giving you a more private surfing experience.

7. chat Apps: Well-liked chat services like Skype, Facebook Messenger, and WhatsApp function well in Maryland. You may use them to send messages, make phone and video calls, and remain in touch with loved ones by using Wi-Fi or mobile data.

8. Emergency Services: Call 911 for quick help in case of an emergency. The emergency response personnel can converse in English and provide the necessary assistance.

When accessing private or sensitive information, keep public Wi-Fi security in mind. Use HTTPS-secured websites wherever possible, and stay away from using unprotected networks to access sensitive accounts or share personal data.

Because cell networks and Wi-Fi access points are so widely available in Maryland, keeping connected is typically simple.

Respect for local customs and manners

It's crucial to respect local customs and observe local etiquette while visiting Maryland. Following are some general principles:

1. civility: Marylanders appreciate civility and politeness. When speaking with locals, whether in restaurants, stores, or casual settings, use the words "please" and "thank you."

2. Punctuality: In Maryland, being on time is valued. Respect other people's time by being on time for appointments, meetings, and social events.

3. Personal Space: When talking with others, particularly those you don't know well, respect personal space and keep your distance.

4. Tipping: In Maryland, tipping is traditional. Tipping is expected of service employees

including waiters, waitresses, bartenders, cab drivers, and hotel workers. 15% to 20% of the entire cost is usually the customary gratuity.

5. Queuing: It's crucial to wait your turn and preserve order in public locations where queues occur, such as ticket lines or lines for public transit.

6. Maryland is a state with a diversified population in terms of culture. Accept and value the variety of its inhabitants, including their many languages, cultures, and customs.

7. Dress Code: Choose modest clothing that fits the occasion. Although there isn't a strict dress code in Maryland, it's best to dress up for business meetings, formal occasions, or religious locations.

8. Environmental Awareness: Be aware of your impact on the environment and recycle and dispose of rubbish according to the rules. Don't leave trash in public spaces and keep them tidy.

9. Photography: It's courteous to get someone's consent before taking their picture, particularly if they are a stranger.

10. Local Laws and Regulations: To ensure that you abide by local laws and regulations throughout your vacation, familiarize yourself with them. Examples include driving laws, smoking bans, and alcohol consumption restrictions.

Keep in mind that Maryland is a diversified state that has a mixture of urban, suburban, and rural locations. Depending on the area and culture, customs and expectations may change. Making your stay pleasurable and productive will be made possible by exercising respect, being open-minded, and being mindful of others.

Maryland essentials for packing

Take into account the following necessities while preparing for a vacation to Maryland:

1. Clothes: Bring clothes appropriate for the weather and the activities you want to do. Maryland has all four seasons, so be sure to dress appropriately. If you want to visit beaches or pools throughout the summer, pack breathable, lightweight clothes as well as swimwear. Pack several warm layers for the winter, such as sweaters, jackets, and a coat. Don't forget to carry a pair of comfortable walking or trekking shoes.

2. Weather Protection: Because of the unpredictability of Maryland's weather, it is a good idea to pack things for weather protection. Carry an umbrella or a thin raincoat in case there are sudden downpours. Pack sunscreen, a hat, and sunglasses if you want to travel in the summer for sun protection.

3. Travel papers: Double-check that you have all required travel papers, including your passport (if you're traveling internationally), a valid driver's license or other form of identification, and any necessary tickets or reservations. It's a smart idea to save both digital and hard copies safely on your phone or on the cloud.

4. Electronics: Pack any necessary electronics, including your phone, a charger, and any other gadgets you may need. To keep your electronics charged while you're on the move, think about a portable power bank. Check to see whether you need a power adaptor to connect your electronics into American outlets if you are going from another nation.

5. Prescription Drugs and First Aid: Bring any prescription drugs you may need along with a basic first aid kit that includes bandages, painkillers, and any other drugs or medical supplies you may need.

6. Personal care items: Pack travel-sized versions of your toothbrush, toothpaste, shampoo, conditioner, soap, and any other personal care products you may need. Make sure these products adhere to TSA restrictions if you're traveling by air.

7. Money and Payment Options: Bring enough USD currency with you to cover any urgent needs. Bring credit/debit cards with you as well for bigger transactions and emergencies. To prevent any card problems while you're abroad, think about telling your bank about your vacation intentions.

8. Travel adapters: Bring the proper travel adapter to plug in your electronic gadgets if you're coming from a nation with different electrical outlets.

9. Snacks and Water Bottle: Bring some snacks and a reusable water bottle for on-the-go hydration and to stay energetic while on your activities.

10. Miscellaneous Items: Depending on your own requirements and preferences, think about bringing along additional necessities like a travel pillow, earplugs, a reusable shopping bag, a camera, a guidebook or map, and any particular gear you'll need for your scheduled activities (such as beach towels, hiking equipment, etc.).

Before you pack, be sure to check the weather forecast to make sure you're ready for the circumstances where you're going. It's a good idea to pack lightly and allow space in your luggage for any souvenirs or other goods you may buy while traveling.

Printed in Great Britain
by Amazon